STARTING

FROM

SEED

The Natural

Gardener's Guide

to Propagating

Plants

D0958482

FOR THE
ADVANCE
MENT OF
BOTANY
AND THE
SERVICE OF
THE CITY

BROOKLYN
BOTANIC
GARDEN
PUBLICATIONS
· MCMXCVIII ·

Janet Marinelli
SERIES EDITOR

Jane Ludlam
MANAGING EDITOR

Bekka Lindstrom
ART DIRECTOR

Stephen K·M. Tim
VICE PRESIDENT, SCIENCE, LIBRARY & PUBLICATIONS

Judith D. Zuk
PRESIDENT

Elizabeth Scholtz
DIRECTOR EMERITUS

STARTING FROM SEED

THE NATURAL GARDENER'S GUIDE TO PROPAGATING PLANTS

Karan Davis Cutler-Guest Editor

Handbook #157
Copyright © Winter 1998 by the Brooklyn Botanic Garden, Inc.
Handbooks in the *21st-Century Gardening Series,* formerly *Plants & Gardens,*
are published quarterly at 1000 Washington Ave., Brooklyn, NY 11225.
Subscription included in Brooklyn Botanic Garden subscriber membership dues ($35.00 per year).
ISSN # 0362-5850   ISBN # 1-889538-09-4
Printed by Science Press, a division of the Mack Printing Group

◨ **TABLE OF CONTENTS** ◨

STARTING FROM SEED

🔲

by Karan Davis Cutler

IN 1989, I VISITED the late Father John Fiala, an amateur hybridizer best known for breeding lilacs and flowering crabapples (his definitive books on those two ornamentals, *Lilacs: The Genus Syringa* and *Flowering Crabapples: The Genus Malus*, were published by Timber Press). It was August, and as we walked through his Ohio garden, Father Fiala pulled seed pods off one lilac bush after another: "Try planting them," he said, "you may get something interesting."

What I got, nine years later, was better than interesting: three long rows of 10-foot lilac bushes, about 60 altogether, with flowers ranging from white to deep purple, each producing a new generation of seeds. Nothing was so wonderful that I considered buying a new grafting knife and becoming a commercial lilac grower, but my lilacs are handsome and fragrant enough to enhance any landscape. And they *will* enhance my landscape as soon as I make time to move them out of my vegetable garden.

Nine years may be a longer timetable than you have in mind when you cover a seed with a bit of soil. But my lilac bushes certainly confirm that those brown parchment seeds—looking like tiny dried lanceolate

"I've got to get some

seeds, right away.

Nothing's planted.

I don't have a thing in

the ground."

WILLY LOMAN, IN ARTHUR MILLER'S
Death of a Salesman, 1949

❦   ❦   ❦

Using seeds to plant a kitchen garden of heirloom vegetables, such as this one at the Seed Savers Exchange Heritage Farm in Decorah, Iowa, helps preserve the planet's botanical riches.

Seeds come in many shapes and forms. The elliptical seeds of this 'Sun Bright' sunflower are edible, not only for humans but also for animals, and are also used as a drying oil.

leaves—were remarkable things! The 19th-century American author Henry David Thoreau, no stranger to the natural world, also was impressed: "I have great faith in a seed. . . . Convince me that you have a seed there, and I am prepared to expect wonders."

You, too, can expect wonders from seeds. They come in an army of sizes, from the dustlike specks of epiphytic orchids to the 40-pound monsters produced by the double coconut (*Lodoicea seychellarum*). And in all sorts of forms: the silky tailed seeds of milkweed; the striped or black elliptical seeds of sunflowers; the round, roofed seeds of oaks; the nearly square seeds of corn; the rock-hard round pits of cherries; the ridged oval seeds of carrots; and tens of thousands more.

However different in form, color, and girth, each seed contains a plant-in-waiting. It is more amazing than a genie in a bottle, as New Englander Celia Thaxter wrote in 1894: "In this tiny casket lie folded roots, stalks, leaves, buds, flowers, seed-vessels . . . all that goes to make up a plant which is as gigantic in proportion to the bounds that confine it as the oak is to the acorn."

There are acres of good reasons to begin with seeds, in addition to the fun of being able to point to mature lilacs or a row of heirloom 'Black Valentine' beans and say, "I grew those from seeds." For one thing, starting plants from seeds is a money-saver: You can pay $5 or more for a six-pack of 'Princess Victoria Louise' oriental poppy seedlings, or $5 for a quarter ounce of seeds, enough to produce 25,000 'Princess Victoria Louise' plants.

Seeds are the only way a home gardener has real access to the world's storehouse of available species and cultivars. Garden centers typically offer only one or two choices, but dozens, even hundreds more are available if you're willing to start with seeds—and to shop by mail. It's not only heirloom cultivars that you won't find at your local nursery, it's regional cultivars and even those plants introduced three or four years ago that have been superseded by something new. "Here today, gone tomorrow" is a phrase that could have been invented for seed-company inventories. Fortunately, there are specialized seed firms, small, independent seed companies, and seed-saving organizations—many are listed in "Seed Sources" (page 92)—that give gardeners a chance to grow something other than mainstream cultivars.

By growing unique or heirloom cultivars or strains, by increasing stands of beleaguered species, you become a steward of our planet's botanical riches. Planting from seeds—and saving and sharing those seeds—is a crucial part of the preservation of Spaceship Earth, as the American futurist Buckminster Fuller called the planet.

Few gardeners take the commitment to protect and maintain our botanical heritage more seriously than do the members of the Seed Savers Exchange and the Flower & Herb Exchange, the largest seed-preservation organizations in the United States. As crucial as this work is, it isn't a grim undertaking, and among the benefits of being an SSE or F&HE member is the right to purchase or trade for seeds grown by other members.

Sharing seeds—becoming what an 18th-century Englishman called "Brothers of the Spade"—is a joyous and companionable, even intimate, experience, as these entries from the latest SSE and F&HE yearbooks make clear.

• From an Indiana gardener willing to share bean and tomato seeds: "An extremely wet spring set planting back 5 weeks, so most of the limas and runners did not mature. I did get about 60 varieties of pole beans and tomatoes planted. All tomatoes have been fermented, washed, and air dried."

• An Illinois gardener, who offers seeds of 271 tomato cultivars, adds: "'Eva Purple Ball' seed sent out last year may have been crossed or mixed. If you got some, let me know so I can send you a pure sample."

• A California gardener explains: "I had a very bad year due to health problems. All requests not filled yet will be filled eventually. I apologize for the delay. Thank you."

• From a Maryland gardener offering cowpeas, limas, sweet potatoes, and tomatoes: "To the gentleman who ordered 'Woods Prolific' bush lima—I am sorry I lost your letter, so if you will send me your address next spring, I will send you the seed."

• A warning from a Mississippi gardener with bean, collard, corn, cowpea, cucumber, eggplant, gourd, millet, mustard, okra, pepper, and squash seeds—156 varieties in all: "Due to two hurricanes, okra plants were laid down and it was impossible to hand-pollinate. May have been some mixing of varieties."

• A New Yorker writes: "Does anyone want some garlic escapees from the National Plant Germplasm Center naturalized in Geneva, NY? I gathered seed from flowering stalks. Can send half-sibs if someone has a Mendelian bent."

• From an Oklahoma member with collard, melon, mustard, okra, onion, squash, and tomato seeds to share: "I am collecting pink and purple tomatoes. If you have a good one that you would like me to try here in Oklahoma, send a small sample. I will let you know how they did in a hot, dry climate."

The chapters that follow will give you a fuller picture of seeds—their biology and chemistry, their political, social, and environmental significance, as well as directions on how best to grow, harvest, and store them. Even with good directions, however, planting seeds isn't foolproof. Sometimes they don't come up. Sometimes they fall prey to disease, insects, or animal pests. Sometimes they aren't what you expect. According to humorists Henry Beard and Roy McKie's *Gardening: A Gardener's Dictionary* (1982), seeds are a "costly, but highly nutritious form of bird food sold in handsome packets printed with colorful pictures of flowers and vegetables."

All gardeners experience failures, so don't let one bad result discourage you. Nine times out of ten, your results will be stellar. As Ruth Page wrote in *Gardening Journal* (1989): "Remember, nature has designed [seeds] to *want* to grow. You and the garden seeds have exactly the same goal—what could be more reassuring."

And what could be more reassuring than this offering from an Indiana gardener and Seed Savers Exchange member: "I suffered two more mini strokes in mid-October, which kept me from harvesting seeds from tomatoes and peppers that I had just picked and boxed to save. I'm just listing one pimento and hoping for a better year."

That's the nice thing about sowing seeds: There's always a better year. ◙

SEED SPECIFICS

◩

by Peter Loewer

FORTUNATELY, A PH.D. IN BOTANY or genetics isn't necessary to grow plants successfully from seed. But this chapter on seed basics will help you better understand what seeds are, where they come from, their role in plant reproduction, and why they are so critical to the health and survival of plant species. It will also help you appreciate—the next time you head for the pumpkin patch, perennial border, fields, or woods—the wonders of these typically tiny parcels of life, which contain all the fundamental parts of a mature plant—leaves, stem, and root.

AND THEN THERE WERE SEEDS

Plants didn't always produce seeds. Millions of years ago, when the world was mostly water, swamp, or just plain wet, terrestrial spore-producing plants like ferns and mosses were supreme because they used water to facilitate reproduction. Once the continents began to drift apart and land rose, the earth's climate began to fluctuate. The seasons were born. Seed-bearing plants were one adaptation to these drier conditions. Scientists divide these higher plants into two groups: the gymnosperms

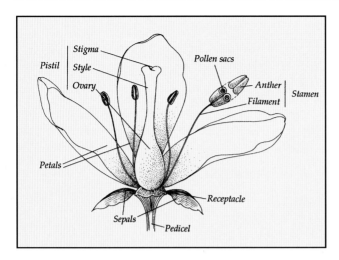

A complete, or perfect, flower contains both a female part—the pistil, usually composed of a stigma, style, and ovary—and male parts—stamens, usually composed of a filament and an anther. An incomplete flower is either male or female.

(*gymno*, meaning naked, and *sperm*, meaning seed), such as pines, firs, and cycads; and the angiosperms (*angio*, meaning contained in a vessel), or flowering plants. Seed-bearing plants, which are of most interest to the majority of gardeners, represent one of the most important steps in the evolution of the plant kingdom.

The life cycle of a gymnosperm is clearly represented by the white pine, *Pinus strobus*. Every spring, pollen-bearing male cones appear at the ends of the tree's lower branches, clustered just below the new crop of needles. When mature, the cones release clouds of pollen, which are carried by the air to the female cones growing at the trees' tops. After being fertilized by the pollen, the individual eggs mature into embryos. That process takes a minimum of 13 months, not including an additional year or so for the seeds to fully develop. Finally, mature and winged, the seeds gently glide to the ground, where they will lie through winter, waiting for spring's warmth to prompt them to germinate.

FABULOUS FLOWERS

About 75 percent of all the seed-bearing plants on earth today are not gymnosperms, but rather angiosperms. All angiosperms produce flowers, which botanists define as "shoots, modified for reproduction." Although gardeners value flowers for their shapes, colors, and fragrance, nature designed them solely as a means of reproduction. As a result, most flowers have similar elements.

First, the typical flower has a *receptacle,* a structure that holds the rest of the floral parts together. Before opening, the flower petals are protected by a *calyx,* an outermost whorl, or ring, made up of modified leaves called *sepals.* A second inner whorl, called the *corolla,* is made up of petals. Collectively, the calyx and corolla are known as the *perianth* of a flower.

Petals are often brightly colored in order to attract insects and birds (a few flowers, such as the poinsettia, appear to have brightly colored petals that actually are modified leaves called *bracts;* in a handful of flowers, such as tulips, these colorful parts are called *tepals,* because it's difficult to determine if they are sepals or petals). Petals can serve as both beacons and landing fields for insects, and many petals even have lines on the surface that act as arrows, leading pollinators to the flower's center.

Inside the whorl of petals are the *stamens,* the male parts of the flower (see illustration, opposite). The typical stamen consists of a long stalk, or *filament,* with a swollen tip called the *anther,* which is the structure that produces grains of pollen. The female part of the flower, known as the *pistil,* usually includes the *stigma,* the sticky portion that traps pollen; the *style,* the stemlike portion that holds the stigma where it can best catch pollen; and the *ovary,* the swollen base of the pistil. Inside the ovary are immature seeds, or *ovules,* waiting to be fertilized.

When flowers have some form of all these parts, they're known as complete. Complete flowers are also known as perfect flowers, because they contain both male and female parts; imperfect flowers have either male or female parts, either stamens or pistil, but not both. Plants, such as sweet corn, squash, and cucumbers, that contain both male and female flowers are called monoecious. When the male and female flowers occur on different plants, as in hollies, asparagus, and persimmons, the plants are called dioecious; to produce flowers—and seeds—you need to have both a male and a female plant in your garden, or at least in the immediate vicinity.

GREEN GENES

Flowers usually must be pollinated for seeds to form. There are two basic kinds of pollination: self-pollination and cross-pollination. Self-pollination occurs when the pollen of a flower fertilizes that same flower or another

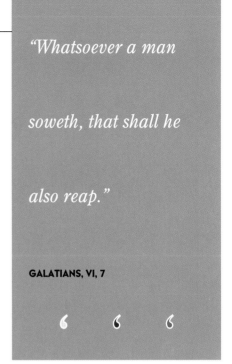

"Whatsoever a man soweth, that shall he also reap."

GALATIANS, VI, 7

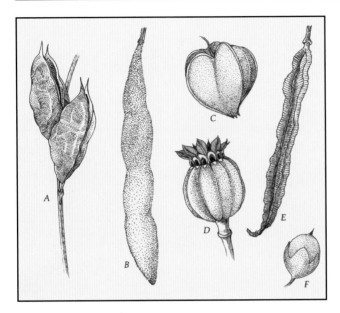

Seed pods come in many different shapes and sizes, such as: false indigo, *Baptisia australis* (A); wisteria, *Wisteria sinensis* (B); husk tomato, *Physalis alkekengi* (C); poppy, *Papaver somniferum* (D); mamane, *Sophora chrysophylla* (E); and flax, *Linum perenne* (F).

flower on the same plant. The typical self-pollinating species has perfect flowers, the ones with both male and female parts. Peas, lettuce, tomatoes, snap beans, and snapdragons are examples of self-pollinating plants; they can be grown from seed without fear of crossings that may result in plants with unwanted variations from the parents.

Cross-pollination results when pollen from one flower fertilizes a flower on another plant. The flowers of cross-pollinating plants can be either perfect or imperfect. The constant mixing of genes that occurs with cross-pollination is crucial in helping species remain healthy and vigorous.

After centuries of observation, we know that cross-pollination is carried out naturally by several types of pollinators. The most important pollinators are the wind, insects, birds, bats, and, finally, water. Wind-pollinated plants normally have no nectar, no fragrance, and no brilliant colors to attract wildlife. Instead, their floral structure is suited to sending and receiving pollen on the breeze. Grasses are a good example; although their flowers are visible, they are tiny.

Plants that are pollinated by insects, birds, bats, and other wildlife tend to have bright, attention-grabbing flowers—real advertisements for themselves. The payoff for the pollinating animals is food: either pollen, which is eaten by some insects, or nectar. Many flowers are specifically designed to accommodate the animals that will pollinate them. The foot-long spurs of the Christmas star orchid depend on a specific moth with a foot-long tongue; the stink of carrion flowers attracts the tiny flies that

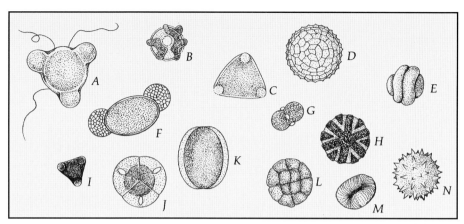

On a microscopic level, pollen can vary greatly from plant to plant: willow (A), dandelion (B), apple (C), ruellia (D), mimulus (E), pine (F), chervil (G), passiflora (H), robinia (I), rhododendron (J), buckwheat (K), acacia (L), geranium (M), and sunflower (N).

transport its pollen; flowers pollinated by bats tend to open at dusk, the same time that bats become active.

We humans are also adept at a specific type of cross-pollination, known as hand-pollination. The objective of hand-pollination is to avoid random cross-breeding—and thus to guarantee that the seeds you save will produce plants like their parents. To insure this, you must prevent insects from visiting the flowers of plants you've selected for seed saving. Then you must perform the insects' job yourself. (For more information about hand-pollination, see "Playing Mother Nature," page 88.)

SEX TO SEEDS

Imagine it's a bright sunny day, somewhere in the temperate zone. The sun is high in a blue sky and a breeze moves across a field of waving grasses and brightly colored wildflowers. You stop at a clump of sundrops, a day-flowering species in the evening primrose family. On top of a two-foot stem, bright yellow, four-petaled flowers are in full bloom. From stage right, enter a bumble bee, his hind legs bright yellow from pollen. The bee buzzes in flight, then spots the flowers. It swoops down and sticks its tongue into the four-pronged stigma at the flower's center. As the bee moves about in a somewhat clumsy way, pollen grains attach themselves to the stigma.

What happens next takes place on the microscopic level. When a grain of pollen becomes attached to the stigma, one of its two cells stimulates

Glacier lily (*Erythronium grandiflorum*) is a living diagram of both the male and female reproductive parts of a flower. The bright yellow, pollen-bearing anthers surround the female organ, the pistil.

the creation of a pollen tube that grows inside the style, creating a path between the stigma and the flower's ovary. Once the tube is complete, the second cell divides into two sperm, which use the pollen tube to reach the ovule. One sperm joins with an egg to create a zygote, a fertilized egg; the second sperm fuses with other nuclei to form the endosperm, a food supply contained in the seed.

As time passes, the zygote becomes the embryo of the new plant. The seeds of flowering plants come in a great variety of sizes, shapes, and textures, but the embryonic plants contained within have the same basic design, with a rudimentary leaf or leaves, called cotyledons, as well as a root tip and a stem. (Cotyledons are the first leaves to appear after a seed sprouts; they are followed by the plant's true leaves.) Most flowering plants have two cotyledons, and thus are called dicotyledons, or dicots. The monocotyledons, or monocots, a smaller group, produce only one seed leaf when they sprout. Plants in the grass family, including corn and grains, are monocots.

In flowering plants, the seed is encased in the ovary, which enlarges into a fruit. The fruit may be red like an apple or a rose hip, green like a

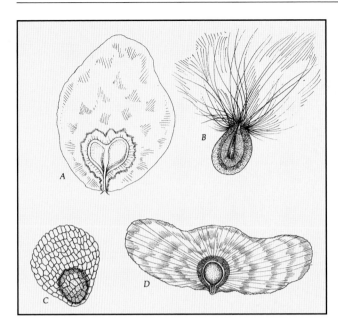

Wind-dispersed seeds often come equipped with wings or plumes to catch the breeze. These include: *Spathodea* species, such as tulip tree (A); *Asclepias* species, such as milkweed (B); *Castilleja* species, such as Indian paintbrush (C), and *Macrozanonia* species, such as *M. macrocarpa* (D).

cucumber, purple like an eggplant, or brown like an acorn. In plants like tomatoes, the fruits become increasingly soft and fleshy as their seeds mature; in other plants, such as garden peas or winter aconite, the fruit wall becomes increasingly dry and eventually splits. Oriental poppies form hard, dry fruits that disperse seeds through small openings like a salt shaker's; other species, such as cherries, have a soft fruit that surrounds a hard pit, or stone, which contains a seed.

No matter what size or shape fruit it is encased in, once the seed, with its embryonic plant, has formed completely, growth stops and the seed typically enters a period of dormancy. The tiny plant consumes minute amounts of energy from food stored inside the seed—just enough to keep it alive, until it germinates and grows.

SPREADING THE TREASURE

After the development of the seeds and fruit, the next order of business for any flowering plant is dispersal—getting the next generation out into the world where it can find suitable habitat to germinate and grow. Anyone who has ever tramped through the woods with a longhaired dog or wearing wool pants knows how some seeds travel: They become affixed to clothing and fur by using hooks, barbs, and even Velcro-like natural structures to guarantee their dispersal around the country, if not the world. The seeds of mistletoe are covered with a sticky substance and

Bees of all types, such as the mining bee on this goldenrod flower, are important pollinators for many types of plants.

become attached to birds and other animals. We humans unintentionally spread seeds in other ways: as discarded foodstuff or as unintentional traveling companions, hidden in pants cuffs, or stuck to the mud on dirty boots and shoes—and we spread them intentionally by buying or collecting seeds and planting them in our gardens.

Plants don't require humans to spread their seeds, however. Small seeds often use the wind to blow them from place to place. Some seeds, like those of orchids, are dustlike; others have plumes, like dandelion or milkweed; or, as do the seeds of maple, they have wings that enable them to glide through the air.

Whether by rain, streams, or ocean currents, many seeds are distributed by water. Very small seeds, especially if they are light in proportion to their size, float. Corky seeds, like those of the carrot family, can stay afloat for weeks.

Seeds are also spread by animals that eat fleshy fruits. The seeds in these fruits often pass through animals' alimentary tracts unharmed; in some cases, the journey through the digestive system even speeds up germination. Beetles, ants, and scores of other insects carry seeds from one location to another. Finally, plants themselves are responsible for

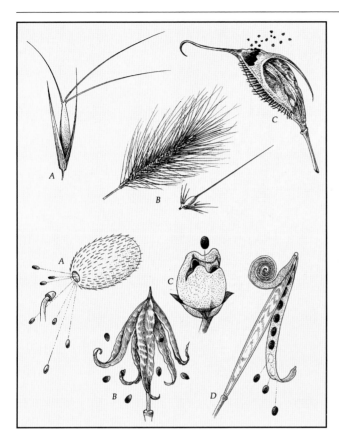

TOP: Seeds that stick to clothing or fur: needle grass, *Aristida oligantha* (A); squirrel grass, *Hordeum jubatum* (B), with one seed at right; and a pod of the unicorn plant, *Proboscidea louisianica* (C), shaking seeds.

BOTTOM: Seeds dispersed by mechanical means: squirting cucumber, *Ecballium elaterium* (A); impatiens, *Impatiens aurella* (B); witchhazel, *Hamamelis virginiana* (C); and *Cardamine hirsuta* (D).

spreading seeds: A number of species, such as the yellow-flowered creeping oxalis, shoot their seeds into the air. The record is probably held by the West Indian swordbean, whose large pods snap open with a crack and propel their seeds at least 20 feet. Less impressive is the squirting cucumber, an annual vine whose fruits push their seeds out in a lump of semi-liquid mucilage. Not neat but effective.

SEED STEADFASTNESS

Wherever they land, seeds can remain in suspended animation until conditions are right to spur germination. While some seeds, given water, will germinate immediately, many others follow an internal clock which insures, as much as possible, that when the seed does germinate, conditions will be conducive to its growth. For example, some seeds require a period of exposure to cold temperatures to break dormancy—nature's way of making sure that seeds of plants in the temperate zone don't germinate until the killing cold of winter has passed. Gardeners need to sim-

Grass flowers disperse their pollen in the wind.

ulate these natural conditions in order to get such seeds to grow. (See "Special Handling," pages 66 through 69.)

The seeds of some plants can remain dormant for months or even years. While the seeds of most species remain viable for only a few years (some for only a few days), others have remarkable longevity. Although many of the tales of sprouting seeds that were found in centuries-old tombs are apocryphal, there is good evidence that some seeds have astonishing durability. The record for longevity probably goes to an Arctic lupine from the Canadian Yukon—seeds germinated after they had been frozen and buried in an ancient rodent burrow for 10,000 years.

Scientists believe that the seed coat is the mechanism that allows a seed to be viable for so long. Typically, this structure consists of an outer and inner cuticle, often impregnated with waxes or fats, which are surrounded by one or more layers of thick-walled, protective cells that are so hard that it is difficult for water to seep into the interior and trigger germination. Sometimes this makes the gardener's job more complicated, requiring special measures to prompt a seed to germinate (some seeds won't germinate until the protective seed coat has been roughed up a bit, as it is when seeds pass through an animal's gut). But mostly, it's a boon, because seeds often must be stored for weeks or months, and in some cases years, before they can be planted.

WHAT'S IN A NAME?

Because plants' reproductive parts are unique characteristics, they have often been used to classify plant species. However, botanists are continually making discoveries, which is one reason that a gardener may suddenly discover that a plant's scientific name has been changed. For example, some botanists have considered species of liverleaf to be members of the genus *Anemone*, while other botanists have classified the same plants as members of the genus *Hepatica*. This controversy dates back over 200 years! However, recent molecular evidence suggests that all liverleaf species should be treated as members of the genus *Anemone*—the eastern North American native sharp-lobed hepatica (*A. acutiloba*), for example.

In general, though, scientific names remain the same from one generation to the next. Many are unchanged from the time of Linnaeus, the Swedish naturalist credited with devising the binomial system of plant nomenclature in the middle of the 18th century. The Linnaean system is used throughout the world, so an American wildflower gardener can be absolutely certain that when she tells an English visitor about her bluebells they both are referring to *Mertensia virginica*, not *Hyacinthoides non-scriptus*, *Campanula rotundifolia*, or another of the additional half dozen plants with the same common name.

Under the Linnaean system, every plant in the wild has a two-part name. The first, the genus name, identifies the group of closely related species to which it belongs; the second part, which is usually descriptive, is the species name, or specific epithet. All oaks, for instance, belong to the genus *Quercus*; red oaks are *Quercus rubra* (rubra, for red).

In addition to the genus and species names, some cultivated plants have additional cultivar names—for example, hybrids that are the result of cross-breeding aimed at producing new characteristics, such as larger flowers, different colors, or disease resistance. According to international rules of botanical nomenclature, the cultivar name should be enclosed in single quotes. Thus, *Quercus rubra* 'Maxima' is a cultivar of *Quercus rubra*, or red oak.

SEEDS & DIVERSITY: EDIBLE PLANTS

by Kent Whealy

EACH SPRING WHEN I AM planting seeds, down on my knees in the warm, fragrant soil, I feel a magical connection with gardeners everywhere. All seeds are ancient, living links in unbroken chains reaching back through time. I cannot possibly comprehend the history contained in the tiny, powerful seeds that I hold in my hands, nor what may come after my brief involvement. Our neolithic ancestors started domesticating plants 10,000 years ago with the simple act of replanting seeds that they had gathered for food. Whenever gardeners save their own seeds, they become part of this ancient tradition.

Because the United States and Canada are nations of immigrants, North American gardeners are blessed with access to a cornucopia of food crops. From every corner of the world, gardeners and farmers brought along their best seeds when they came to this continent. Many of these immigrants were afraid that their seeds might be confiscated upon arrival, so they often hid them in the linings of suitcases or in the hems of dresses. Generation after generation, these living heirlooms have provided fond memories of former lives and have ensured contin-

"He places a seed in

the dust for the reason

That it may in the day

of distress, give fruit."

SADI,
13th-century Persian poet

Immigrant farmers and gardeners bringing seeds from all around the globe have made North America a rich cornucopia of food crops.

ued enjoyment of foods from the old country. This unique heritage, steadily accumulating for almost four centuries, continues today with refugees from Laos, Cambodia, Haiti, and Cuba.

A rich flow of plant material was sorely needed because only a few food crops—sunflowers, Jerusalem artichokes, wild rice, cranberries, blueberries, American grapes, pecans, and black walnuts—are native to North America. Almost all the vegetables and herbs we grow today originated in other countries and were brought here by immigrants or plant explorers. The exceptions, of course, are the crops that were being grown by Native Americans before the Europeans arrived: mainly squash, corn, beans, potatoes, tomatoes, and peppers. These originated in South America and had been spreading northward along trading routes for centuries. Some of these Native American food crops have survived and today are among our most treasured traditional seeds. The fact that these seeds have been made available to us is an exceptional privilege, as many Native Americans are reluctant to share their seeds, believing them to be sacred. And rightfully so, for seeds are the sparks of life that feed us all.

Many heirloom, or handed-down, vegetable varieties are still being maintained by gardeners and farmers in isolated rural areas and ethnic enclaves.

Whenever an extremely remote area is thoroughly searched, we often find a treasure trove of heirloom seeds. This isolation can take various forms, but typically it is geographic. Rugged backwoods areas of the Ozark, Smoky, and

Many heirloom crops, such as these potatoes, have natural resistances to pests and diseases. Without this genetic diversity, the world food supply is at risk from epidemics and infestations.

Appalachian mountains are rich in heirlooms, especially in pockets of poverty where seeds have always been shared rather than purchased. Sometimes isolation is religious and, again, we are privileged to have access to varieties grown and maintained by Mennonite, Amish, and Hutterite gardeners.

Often, heirloom vegetables and fruits have been grown on one farm by different generations of a family for more than 150 years. However, economic pressures are continuing to force young farm families off the land and elderly gardeners can find no one willing to maintain their collections. As the older generation passes away, unless other gardeners come forward to replant their seeds, outstanding varieties become extinct. Their unique genetic characteristics are lost forever and future generations will never enjoy these extinct heirloom varieties.

GENETIC DIVERSITY

About 43 million U.S. families (nearly one of every three Americans) grow part of their own food, while two-thirds of the world's people live on what they are able to grow. Yet the genetic diversity of food crops everywhere is eroding at an unprecedented and accelerating rate. The vegetable and fruit varieties being lost are the result of millions of years of natural selection and 10,000 years of human domestication and adaptation. Each variety is genetically unique and many have natural resistances to the diseases and pests with which they evolved. Plant breeders use these old varieties to breed those resistances into modern food crops, which are continually being attacked by new diseases and pests. Without these infusions of genetic diversity, food production worldwide is at risk from epidemics and infestations.

In the last century, for example, the lack of genetic diversity caused the Irish potato famine. The potato originated in the Andes Mountains of South America, where Indian farmers once grew more than 3,000 varieties. In the mid-1500s, one variety was brought to Europe, and by the 1700s, European diets were dependent on potatoes. Freed from hunger, Ireland's population soared to eight million, twice its present population. Then spores of a South American potato fungus, commonly known as the black rot, reached Ireland in the summer of 1845. The genetically uniform Irish potatoes lacked resistance and rotted in the fields. Six years of famine resulted in more than one million deaths from starvation and forced another million to immigrate to North America.

Similarly, the Southern corn blight of 1970—which destroyed 15 percent of the U.S. corn crop—occurred because six equally susceptible

Gardeners who save their own seeds from even a small kitchen garden with heirloom vegetables can help preserve the genetic diversity of food crops.

varieties accounted for 71 percent of all corn planted. According to *Genetic Vulnerability of Major Crops*, published in 1972 by the National Academy of Sciences, all major American agricultural crops have similarly narrow genetic bases and are susceptible to epidemics, which can occur whenever weather conditions are favorable, the crop is genetically vulnerable, and an insect or disease is present.

Agronomists have no control over the weather, the appearance of new pests, nor disease-causing microorganisms. What they do have are vast storehouses of genetic material, which have allowed them to exert considerable control over the genetic makeup of our food crops. However, much of the irreplaceable genetic diversity stored in seed banks around the world is not being regenerated. It is rapidly dying out just when our food crops are becoming ever more uniform and vulnerable, the result of agriculture's dependence on vast plantings of genetically uniform plants (called "monocultures") grown on ever-larger farms. For example, new apple orchards are being planted almost exclusively with 'Red Delicious' and a half dozen other varieties that were bred mainly for appearance, long-term storage, and long-distance shipping.

The same forces that are eroding our vegetable resources down to a few monocultures are causing other widespread losses. Vegetables and fruits that could be produced locally by small growers using organic methods are grown instead on factory-farms in California or Florida, sprayed repeatedly with toxic chemicals, and then shipped across the country. Americans consume an average of three pounds of food additives and pesticide residues each year, and the water we drink is increasingly poisoned by agricultural herbicides, pesticides, and chemical fertilizers. Irradiated and genetically engineered foods are unlikely to be labeled as such. Increasingly, the only way to be certain that our families are consuming wholesome food is to grow it ourselves.

SEED COMPANIES: LOSSES & GAINS

Home gardeners are especially affected by the decrease in seed diversity caused by consolidation within the seed industry. These losses peaked between 1984 and 1987, when 54 out of the remaining 230 North American seed companies either went out of business or were taken over. Multinational agrichemical conglomerates went on a buying spree, purchasing smaller companies and dropping their regionally adapted collections of standard, or nonhybrid, vegetables.

About six percent of all vegetable varieties are dropped from seed catalogs every year, which means that two-thirds of the nearly 5,000 nonhybrid varieties offered in 1984 were gone by 1994. The varieties that are dropped often represent the life's work of several generations of gardeners or breeders, were adapted to regional climates, and were resistant to local diseases and pests.

These losses have the greatest impact on backyard gardeners, because almost all vegetable breeding today is intended to help commercial farmers. The agrichemical conglomerates have replaced the nonhybrid vegetables with more profitable hybrids and patented varieties that grow well throughout the country. Modern agricultural crops are bred for same-day ripening to facilitate harvesting by machines and for tough skins and solid flesh that can withstand long-distance shipping. Such cultivars seldom suit the needs of home gardeners, who are rightfully concerned with flavor and tenderness, and want fruits and vegetables that will ripen over an extended period.

Home gardeners should know that heirloom vegetables are the best varieties they will ever see. Far from being obsolete or inferior, these are the cream of our crops. Each is unique and irreplaceable. If this heritage is allowed to die out, home growers will become dependent on the generic and hybrid varieties offered by multinational seed companies. And that means not only giving up our right to determine the quality of the food we grow and consume, but losing the ability to save our own seeds, which is how most of this incredible diversity came to exist and will help insure its continued survival.

A decade ago it was already apparent that the loss of vegetable varieties could be partially offset if specialized seed companies continued to emerge and offer unique collections. Today the heirloom seed movement in the United States continues to gain momentum, a bright ray of hope in an otherwise bleak situation. Between 1991 and 1994, small alternative seed companies introduced nearly 1,800 varieties that had never before been commercially available, including many heirloom, Native American, foreign, and regionally adapted varieties. A mere 21 companies are responsible for offering more than half of these "new" varieties, so the gains are fragile. Home gardeners should encourage and support this promising trend by patronizing these exceptional companies. (See "Seed Sources," page 92.)

Members of the Seed Savers Exchange, an organization that I founded and direct, currently volunteer their time and energy to maintain more than 20,000 rare vegetable varieties, many with fascinating histories: beans that came over on the *Mayflower*, corn and beans carried by the Cherokee over the Trail of Tears, lettuces grown in Thomas Jefferson's garden at Monticello, and tomatoes that General Lee sent home during the Civil War. Equally fascinating are the endangered seeds currently flowing across recently opened borders throughout Eastern Europe and the former Soviet Union. These traditional food crops include plant material unlike anything we have ever seen: black tomatoes from Russia, tomatoes with foliage similar to carrot tops, and amazingly short-season melons and watermelons from Siberia. We are truly blessed to be gardeners living here, in this time.

Why should we care about heirloom varieties, and possibly consider becoming involved in their preservation? Because they are our heritage as gardeners. Because they are the richness on the dinner plate of life. Ironically, today's gardeners have access to the greatest array of the best vegetable varieties ever developed, and many of these vegetables remain in immediate danger of being permanently lost. Backyard gardeners are emerging as the most vitally concerned stewards of this irreplaceable genetic wealth. More of us must accept that responsibility. Whenever any of this beautiful, fragile diversity is lost, it is gone. Extinction is forever.

HEIRLOOM SAMPLER

'RED VALENTINE' BEAN. A Native American variety, this bean was "discovered" by Europeans in the early 1800s and taken to Europe, where it collected a handful of names. In the 1830s, it recrossed the Atlantic and was first sold by Pennsylvania seedsman David Landreth, who offered it as 'Red Valentine'.

'STOWELL'S EVERGREEN' SWEET CORN. A cross made by Nathan Stowell of Burlington, New Jersey, about 1845, the "evergreen" in the name comes from the fact that plants can be pulled before their ears are ripe, hung upside down in a cool location, and harvested into the winter.

'TALL TELEPHONE' PEA. Famous for its towering vines—eight feet and up—and huge crop of large pods, 'Tall Telephone' was named after Alexander Graham Bell's invention, but home gardeners suspect that the name comes from the need for a support as hefty as a telephone pole to hold up the heavy vines.

'MARTIN'S CARROT' HOT PEPPER. A long, orange, carrot-like Mennonite heirloom, developed in the 19th century, 'Martin's Carrot' is named for the Ephrata, Pennsylvania, family who preserved it. Moderately hot, it is known as *Mordipeffer* among Old Order Mennonites.

'QUAKER PIE' PUMPKIN. A Quaker heirloom from New York, this pumpkin was introduced by W. Atlee Burpee & Company in 1888. Its popularity has been limited, probably because of its unusual white flesh.

'HUBBARD' SQUASH. Considered an "American" variety, this 10-pound, dark green, yellow-fleshed winter squash originally came from the West Indies and was introduced in the United States in the 1840s. Its name honors Elizabeth Hubbard, who introduced it to Massachusetts seedsman James J. H. Gregory.

'BRANDYWINE' TOMATO. The most revered of all old tomatoes, 'Brandywine' is probably a 19th-century commercial variety, not an Amish family heirloom. Its history doesn't mar the flavor of this pink-skinned fruit, however, which is considered superior to all other tomatoes'.

SEEDS & DIVERSITY:
NATIVE PLANTS

by Heather McCargo

OR TOO LONG, much of North America's indigenous flora was overlooked by gardeners in favor of exotic plants from around the globe. During the past few decades, however, this situation has begun to change. As more and more wild habitats are lost and the public becomes concerned about the increasing number of threatened species, the demand for native plants has risen dramatically.

The growing interest in indigenous species and natural landscaping bodes well for the continent's native plant life. But it also poses some problems. Populations of some spectacular but difficult-to-propagate species such as trilliums and orchids are imperiled by unscrupulous collectors and commercial sellers who dig them up from the wild. The growing popularity of herbal remedies is decimating wild populations of plants such as ginseng *(Panax quinquefolius)* and goldenseal *(Hydrastis canadensis)*. In addition, the nursery industry's overreliance on "superior cultivars" of some ornamental natives poses a threat to these species' genetic diversity. What's more, as the nursery business becomes increasingly national, plants frequently are shipped from one region of the country to the next,

"There are no green

thumbs or black

thumbs.

There are only

gardeners and

non-gardeners."

HENRY MITCHELL,
The Essential Earthman,
1981

The best way for gardeners to safe-guard wild natives is to propagate them from seed collected from local plants, such as these sumac and prairie wildflowers in Decorah, Iowa.

Some native plants, such as lady slipper orchids, are difficult to propagate, as their reproduction biology is not clearly understood.

which could create genetic problems for native species. If the regional gene pool of a particular plant is swamped by the genes of its relatives from another part of the country, the resulting offspring could be weaker—less tolerant of cold, drought, or local pests, for example. For native plant gardeners who have no regional nurseries producing plants from local stock, this is a real dilemma: Is it better to purchase a native plant from another part of the country, or substitute an exotic plant instead? The best way for gardeners to safeguard wild populations and the genetic integrity of natives is to propagate them from seed collected from local plants.

NATURAL SELECTION

Genetic diversity in wild plants is extremely important for several reasons. Wild ecosystems are in a constant state of flux because, for one thing, the world's climate is always changing, even without human interference. Genetic diversity within a species provides the best opportunity for a plant to adapt to changing conditions and survive over time. In the wild, most plants reproduce sexually—that is, by seed. Sexual reproduction results in variation among individuals, which means that individuals will differ in their abilities to cope with drought, excessive rain, cold, heat, pollution, and disturbance. If our native flora is to survive into the

The seeds of some species, such as trilliums, take two years to germinate. These and native orchids are imperiled by commercial sellers who dig them up from the wild.

future, it will need genetic diversity to aid in the process of evolution.

The selective pressures on wild plants are different from those on plants in cultivation. In the wild, a plant's flower and seed characteristics reflect the species' mode of fertilization and dispersal—not a human being's conception of beauty. For example, seed ripening and dispersal may happen rapidly, with all the seeds exploding from their pods at once, or more slowly over a period of weeks or months. The seeds of many wild species need a cold period to break dormancy; in some cases, it may take two years or even more for the first shoot to emerge. These various reproductive strategies help ensure that at least some of the seeds germinate when growing conditions are favorable.

Conventional horticulture tends to tamper with a plant's reproductive strategies. Unfortunately, characteristics that are "ornamental" to humans may also make the plant less fit. This can happen intentionally, through breeding to develop more rapid and uniform ripening and germination of seed, or unintentionally, by favoring individuals or varieties that reproduce and flourish in a garden environment rather than in an uncultivated landscape. Horticultural fashion can also alter genetic diversity in plants through selection of cultivars with traits like compactness of growth or double flowers (which usually are sexually dysfunctional). A good example is the popular New England aster cultivar *Aster novae-angliae* 'Purple

Many of the most beautiful native plants and flowers are remarkably easy to grow from seed. Wild columbine seeds are simple to germinate—they require no pre-treatment and grow best when they are sown outdoors in early spring.

Dome', grown for its compact, mounded habit as well as its vibrant purple flowers. In order to be sure of getting the parent's desirable traits, it is usually necessary to propagate cultivars such as 'Purple Dome' vegetatively, typically by rooting cuttings, which means that the new plants are genetically identical—clones. Cloning by definition restricts variation in a plant's gene pool. Even seed-propagated cultivars such as *Echinacea purpurea* 'Magnus', a purple coneflower named "Perennial of the Year" by the Perennial Plant Association, have little genetic diversity; in order to ensure that these plants "come true" when grown from seed, breeders must eliminate most variation in the gene pool through repeated back-crossing. The limited genetic base of both clones and seed-propagated cultivars increases the chances of inbreeding and can threaten the species' long-term health and survival. While the natural habitat and wild populations of *Echinacea purpurea* diminish, cultivars like 'Magnus' do little to contribute to the genetic diversity of the species.

Much of the demand for native plants today is from ecologists and designers doing habitat restoration and gardeners creating naturalistic landscapes. In either case, the hope is that, once established, the plants will grow and reproduce with minimal human intervention. If these plants are to flourish in their naturalistic settings and even augment the gene pools of shrinking native populations, it is especially important to ensure that they are genetically diverse. Hence they should be propagated by seed, preferably from plants in your own region.

PROPAGATION TIPS

You don't need expensive or sophisticated equipment to grow natives from seed. Seeds can be germinated outdoors in beds or flats. In fact, germination outdoors, as opposed to indoors in greenhouses, is in many ways preferable. Seeds sown outside, responding to the local environment, will germinate when soil temperatures are optimum for each species, which can vary from the frosty temperatures of early spring to the heat of midsummer. Seeds that require cold stratification, or a period of exposure to cold temperatures, are satisfied by the freeze and thaw of our cold temperate winters, and seeds that must be sown fresh will not be thrown off their natural cycle by the artificial climate of a greenhouse.

Many native plants, especially the herbaceous perennials, have a reputation for being difficult to germinate because horticulturists traditionally have not understood seed dormancy and germination requirements. Some natives, such as lady slipper orchids *(Cypripedium* species) are indeed difficult to propagate because their reproduction biology is still something of a mystery. But many species are easy to germinate. Following are several procedures, based on the germination requirements for various species, that I've found successful.

No pretreatment
Seeds that need no pretreatment can be stored dry in the refrigerator and sown outdoors in early spring. These include:
Aquilegia canadensis, Wild columbine
Arisaema triphyllum, Jack-in-the-pulpit
Asclepias tuberosa, Butterfly weed
Aster species, Asters
Liatris species, Blazingstars
Solidago species, Goldenrods

Cold stratification
Seeds that require exposure to a period of cold to germinate can be sown outdoors in late fall. These include:

Dutchman's breeches and some other native plants disperse their seeds so quickly that the best way to propagate them is to plant a few specimens, let new plants sprout naturally nearby, and then transplant the seedlings.

Anemonella thalictroides, Rue anemone
Cornus canadensis, Bunchberry
Dodecatheon meadia, Shooting star
Penstemon species, Beardtongues
Sarracenia purpurea, Common pitcher plant
Tiarella species, Foamflowers
Vernonia noveboracensis, Ironweed
Viola species, Violets

Immediate sowing
Some seeds need to be sown immediately upon ripening. If the seeds are allowed to dry out, they usually will not germinate. Most of these species' seeds ripen from late spring through summer and germinate the following spring. These include:
Actaea pachypoda, White baneberry
Caltha palustris, Marsh marigold

Continues on page 38

COLLECTING NATIVE SEED

Acquiring native seed can be a challenge because seed of many species is not yet commercially available, especially seed of local genetic stock (some sources of native seeds are included in the list beginning on page 92). Therefore, gardeners sometimes have no choice but to go out and collect the seed themselves. Here are five guidelines for collecting seed in the wild which can insure that the genetic diversity of native plants is preserved and wild populations are not depleted:

1 Make sure that you have properly identified the species when it is in bloom and have checked with your state Natural Heritage Program to make sure that it is not listed as an endangered or otherwise protected species. Never collect seed from protected species!

2 Always get permission from the landowner before collecting seed.

3 Look for large, healthy populations of the desired species and collect seed from a large number of individuals. If possible, collect seed from several populations in your area to minimize inbreeding. Make sure the seed is ripe before collecting because immature seed often isn't very viable.

4 Never collect more than 5 percent of the seed in any population. If seed set is poor, or if there are a small number of individuals, do not collect the seed.

5 Research the germination requirements of each species before collecting to make sure that you are handling the seed properly and not wasting it.

For more on collecting and storing seed, see page 80.

Clintonia species, Clintonias
Anemone (Hepatica) species, Hepaticas

Time
Some species take two years to germinate, including:
Polygonatum species, Solomon's seals
Smilacina racemosa, False Solomon's seal
Trillium species, Trilliums
Uvularia species, Merrybells

Natural dispersal in a growing bed
In some instances, species that disperse their seeds quickly or whose
seeds are carried off by ants are easiest to handle if you grow a few speci-
mens and let their seed disperse naturally into the garden bed, then
transplant the seedlings into pots. These include:
Asarum canadense, Canadian wild ginger
Dicentra cucullaria, Dutchman's breeches
Jeffersonia diphylla, Twinleaf
Mertensia virginica, Virginia bluebells
Sanguinaria canadensis, Bloodroot
Stylophorum diphyllum, Celandine poppy

Alternating warm and cold
Some species need a warm, moist period of approximately 3 months followed by cold stratification to germinate. In the Northeast, these seeds
can be sown outdoors in mid-summer and will germinate the following
year. In warmer climates, the seeds can be sown in early fall (when the
seed naturally ripens), and the mild autumn temperatures will suffice as
the initial warm period. These species include black cohosh (*Cimicifuga
racemosa)* and meadow lily (*Lilium canadense).*

This chapter includes propagation tips for many common native wildflowers. Information on germination of other native species can be found
in references listed on pages 100 to 101.

After sowing, cover all seed flats with a thin layer of coarse sand. This
helps prevent the seeds from drying or splashing out in the rain. If
rodents are a problem, cover the flats with wire screen. Because some
species can take a year or more to germinate, monitoring for weeds is
important. Locate flats of these species in the shade, where weeds will be
less of a problem.   🔳

SEEDS & DIVERSITY:
HEIRLOOM
FLOWERS

⟨⟩

by Marilyn Barlow

FLOWERS—THEY ARE MADE SOLELY TO gladden the heart of man, for a light to his eyes, for a living inspiration of grace to his spirit, for a perpetual admiration." So elegant and florid, this quote comes from the Victorian-era seed catalog of Comstock, Ferre & Co.

Many of the flowers that captured the hearts and souls of gardeners back then are still in favor today, including morning glories and nasturtiums. However, others have quietly disappeared from gardens and are rarely found in seed catalogs—flowers such as azure-blue single 'Emperor William' cornflower and sweetly scented white marvel-of-Peru. Still others, endangered or perhaps lost, may survive only in print in the lists and descriptions of seed catalogs of the past.

Within the aged covers of these catalogs, one finds a celebration of diversity. The Burpee *Farm Annual* of 1903, for example, lists over 600 annual flower varieties suitable for the garden, including 87 sweet peas. Today, seeds of fewer than 200 annual flowers are offered by the same company, and the emphasis has changed from species to hybrid series.

The simple flower mignonette (*Reseda odorata*) alone was deemed

While some heirloom flowers are still abundant today, old varieties are rapidly disappearing from current seed lists and many exist only in the pages of antique seed catalogs.

worthy of 11 separate listings in Burpee's 1903 issue: 'Machet' (available today), 'New Golden Machet', 'Improved Golden Queen', 'Allan's Defiance', 'Erfurt', 'Quaker City', 'Giant Flowered Red', 'Parson's White Tree', 'Giant Pyramidal', 'Improved Sweet', and 'Giant White Spiral'. To that list, Park's 1904 *Floral Guide* added two more, 'Goliath' and 'Victoria'. One satisfied customer was prompted to write, "Mr. Park, Oh, the delightful fragrance and the modest beauty that lay dormant in a packet of your large-flowered Sweet Mignonette seeds!"

PRESERVING ANTIQUE FLOWERS

In tantalizing prose, period catalogs sing the praises of one antique flower after another: the moonflower's "rich Jessamine-like odor," the cypress vine's "elegant feathery foliage" and "scarlet flowers which stand out like constellations of stars." No wonder we're unable to resist their admonition, "Let everyone possess themselves of it."

Unfortunately, most heirloom flowers have disappeared from commerce. And it's not only venerable old-timers that fashion is passing by. Antique as well as newer varieties continue to drop out of seed production and, therefore, seed catalogs at an alarming rate.

Once an antique flower is rediscovered, period catalogs provide the

At Monticello, Thomas Jefferson's estate in Virginia, gardeners help preserve antique varieties by growing the same plants—such as hollyhocks, other flowers, and vegetables—that Jefferson, an avid gardener, grew himself.

means to authenticate it. Trialing, or growing the variety and comparing it with as may written descriptions and illustrations as possible, is also necessary. If all goes well, these varieties end up in the seed stock and catalog of my company, Select Seeds, and those of other heirloom seed merchants around the world, ready to flourish again. (For a list of these seed sources, see page 92.)

Searching for antique annuals is not the exclusive province of heirloom seed merchants, however. Heirloom seed exchanges, horticultural organizations' seed sales, and agricultural market bulletins are additional sources that enable everyone to be a force for preservation.

Seed merchants and gardeners can join forces to preserve our floral heritage. We can protect antique varieties from the vagaries of large commercial seed houses by enlisting experienced gardeners around the country to obtain seed and become contract growers of these endangered flowers, supplying small seed merchants who, in turn, supply the growing numbers of gardeners enamored of these precious plants.   🌀

SEED PRESERVATION

IN NORTH AMERICA

[◊]

by David J. Ellis

DURING THE BITTER WINTER of 1941-1942, while the German army besieged the Russian city of Leningrad, nine Russian botanists starved to death at the city's Vavilov Institute, perhaps the oldest and most famous seed bank in the world. The scientists died while surrounded by millions of seeds—including rice, corn, oats, wheat, and peas—that they refused to eat because many represented the last known seeds of their variety.

Fortunately, nothing as singularly altruistic has been demanded of seed savers in North America. There is, nonetheless, a long and proud tradition of seed preservation here, beginning with the Native Americans who domesticated the first North American food crops and continuing with the pioneer farmers who passed precious seeds from one generation to the next. Today, there is a continent-wide government seed-preservation network that uses the latest technologies to store seeds far longer than our ancestors ever dreamed. This bureaucracy is augmented by scores of nonprofit organizations and commercial seed companies, which preserve seeds by more traditional methods, and by millions of gardeners who still save their own seeds from year to year.

> *"From a plant's point of view extra seed is just insurance that some will germinate, but to a gardener the sight of two- or three-year-old packets still partially filled with now-defunct seed is depressing. Dreams that die on the shelf."*
>
> **ROGER B. SWAIN,**
> *The Practical Gardener, 1989*

Heirloom seed companies and seed-preservation organizations regenerate a wide diversity of home garden varieties, such as tomatoes, by open pollination.

SEEDS OF DIVERSITY

Seeds are just one of the forms of living plant tissue, or germplasm, that contain the genetic information from which new plants can be grown. Other forms include leaf and stem cuttings, the eyes of root crops, such as potatoes, and—with the advent of tissue culture—even individual cells. Despite the advances in genetic research that allow plant breeders to manipulate individual crops to remove undesirable characteristics or add beneficial ones, the importance of preserving old and diverse sources of germplasm for both edible and ornamental plants has become clear over the course of the last few decades. (See "Seeds and Diversity: Edible Plants," page 22.)

The federal germplasm system preserves many heirloom seeds, but they are placed in an environment that literally and metaphorically "freezes" them in their evolutionary tracks. This setting effectively prevents them from acquiring resistance to the pests and diseases whose mutation continues unabated. These collections are intended to supply breeders with genetic material from all kinds of plants. Heirloom seed companies and seed-preservation organizations, on the other hand, annually regenerate most of their stock by open pollination. These selections are home garden varieties.

SEEDS IN AMERICA: A BRIEF HISTORY

Scientists are still unraveling the history of Native American use and domestication of food crops, but it is known that the earliest human inhabitants of our continent played an important role in the development of many of the plants—corn, beans, and squash, to name three—we rely upon today. The earliest evidence of crop domestication dates to about 2,500 years ago in Arizona and New Mexico.

Native Americans hastened the spread of seeds throughout North America by trading with neighboring tribes. When the first Europeans settled along the Atlantic coast, the seeds they brought with them made their way into Native American gardens, and Native Americans passed their traditional crops to the Europeans. Thus began an assimilation of culinary traditions that continues to this day.

As the European immigrants moved west, they planted their seeds, shared them with neighbors and relatives, and passed them down to their children. Gradually, through natural selection and human intervention, these flowers, fruits, herbs, and vegetables adapted to the climate, pests, and diseases of their new homeland, evolving into the American heirlooms that are now being "rediscovered" by home gardeners.

Only four years after America proclaimed independence from British

Native Americans domesticated the first North American food crops, including corn, beans, and squash, to name three that we rely upon today.

rule, the new country's first seed company—David Landreth & Son—opened in Philadelphia. In the ensuing years, hundreds of other seed companies have joined the competition for the business of America's eager gardening public. The period from 1850 to the 1940s is generally considered the golden age of gardening. Books written during that time, such as Fearing Burr's *Field and Garden Vegetables of America* (1863), show the amazing diversity of plants that were available to American gardeners—64 beet cultivars, 56 different cabbages, 31 types of celery, and more.

This golden age came to an abrupt halt with the movement toward industrialized farming that developed after World War II. In his book *Heirloom Vegetable Gardening* (Henry Holt and Company, 1997), William Woys Weaver writes, "The most fundamental alteration to the picture arrived in the form of hybrid vegetables—plants that do not produce true seed, therefore obliging the gardener to purchase new seed every year—in the 1940s." The business of seeds also changed radically; today, the majority of the seeds sold throughout the world are hybrids produced by a handful of multinational corporations. The good news is that these 20th-century changes in farming also produced the seed-saving movement and a renaissance of small seed companies, whose offerings are more numerous and diverse than ever.

SEED SAVING IN THE 20TH CENTURY

Until the end of the 19th century, large-scale efforts at seed collection and preservation were mainly reserved for naturalist-explorers like John Bartram and "scientific" farmers like Thomas Jefferson. In his foreword to *Heirloom Vegetable Gardening*, Peter J. Hatch, director of gardens and grounds at Monticello, describes the garden in Jefferson's time as "an Ellis Island for immigrant crops."

The foundation of the current national seed preservation system was laid in 1898, when the Section of Seed and Plant Introduction was established under the U.S. Department of Agriculture. It wasn't until 1946, however, that Congress created several regional plant introduction stations to test and breed both indigenous and exotic plants. In the political climate that presaged the Cold War, it became clear that unrestricted access to international germplasm could no longer be taken for granted, and Congress authorized creation of a national seed storage facility to preserve germplasm from around the world for the future use of plant breeders and other researchers. The result was the National Seed Storage Laboratory (NSSL) in Fort Collins, Colorado, which opened in 1958.

The NSSL is now the heart of the National Plant Germplasm System (NPGS), overseen by the U.S. Department of Agriculture's Agricultural Research Service (ARS). About two thirds of the more than 400,000 different genetic materials—called accessions—in the federal system are stored at Fort Collins, which serves as a backup for germplasm contained in the active collections. In addition, there are seven National Germplasm Repositories located throughout the country, from Hilo, Hawaii, and Mayaguez, Puerto Rico, to Corvallis, Oregon, and Geneva, New York. Along with seeds, these facilities store the genetic material of plants that require cloning—asexual propagation by cuttings or tissue culture—to preserve their unique characteristics. These include berries, fruit and nut trees, and ornamental plants.

Seeds and other germplasm stored in the national system come from a variety of sources. Most are from other active NPGS sites, but deposits also come from botanical gardens, overseas agriculture services, U.S. seed companies, and university researchers. In addition to preserving seeds and other genetic resources, one of the main roles of the NPGS is to make its plant germplasm available to researchers around the world. About half of all distributions are to U.S. government or university scientists, a quarter are to foreign scientists, and the remainder are to U.S. private sector scientists and international agencies. Seeds are not available to private individuals, but information about seeds stored in the U.S. sys-

TOP: Jerusalem artichoke is a native North American food crop that indigenous people were growing when European settlers arrived.

BOTTOM: More native North American food crops—arikara sunflower, winter squash, and Washington arikara squash.

tem is available to anyone through the Germ-plasm Resources Information Network (GRIN), a computer database maintained at the ARS facility in Beltsville, Maryland. (To access the GRIN database, see "For More Information," page 103.)

The collections include native and exotic ornamental species, improved cultivars of fiber, feed, and food crops, wild and weedy relatives of food crops, rare and endangered species, and various mutations of genetic stocks. These materials are stored in the event breeders need them to improve plants and crops in the future.

Many of the accessions are from plants that are now extinct in the wild. Each repository holds plants suited to its climate: tropical plants are maintained in Puerto Rico, Hawaii, and Florida, while Mediterranean plants, such as dates, olives, and citrus fruits, are stored in California. Working collections of seeds are housed at regional plant introduction stations, where researchers actively breed and test new plants. Some plant introduction stations hold hundreds of different plant species; others, such as the Potato Germplasm Introduction Project at Sturgeon Bay, Wisconsin, concentrate on one or two crops.

At the NSSL, most of the seeds are dried to remove excess moisture, sealed in moisture-proof containers, and stored at 0°F. Some seeds that are short-lived or difficult to store undergo cryopreservation: they are stored in or above liquid nitrogen at around –320°F. Seeds are scheduled to be tested for viability every 15 years; any that exhibit a germination rate less than 65 percent are regenerated by growing them out and harvesting the seeds.

Despite its good work, the NPGS has been the target of criticism in recent years. A series of investigative articles published by the Associated Press in 1989 revealed that the agency was chronically underfunded and understaffed. As a result, thousands of accessions had not been tested for viability for more than 20 or 30 years, and many others showed viability lower than the established threshold. Accessions were found to include fewer than the 550 seeds designated as the minimum level, and in some cases, seeds held in active collections were not backed up at the Fort Collins repository. Critics also argued that the federal government should try to regenerate seeds by growing plants where they naturally occur—*in situ*—rather than in seed banks that might be located on the other side of the continent. Efforts to improve the NPGS included an expansion of the NSSL in 1992, which allowed an increase in storage capacity to 1.5 million accessions. However, funding problems continue to plague the agency.

The Canadian equivalent of the NPGS is Plant Gene Resources of Canada (PGRC), established in 1970. The PGRC has recently moved its seed collection to a new facility in Saskatoon, Saskatchewan, and now has space to store more than 200,000 kinds of seeds. Canada also maintains a clonal gene bank in Smithfield, Ontario, for fruit and ornamental plants.

Canadian and American scientists traditionally have worked together closely and often share germplasm. At the moment, the United States is storing apple cuttings from the Canadian system, while Canada is backing up a number of U.S. accessions of small grains such as barley and oats. According to Ken Richards, research manager of PGRC, Canada is in the process of adding information about its germplasm to the GRIN computer database used in the United States. That will put all of North America on one database, he says.

NONGOVERNMENTAL SEED SAVING

Federal governments aren't the only agencies interested in saving the riches contained in the germplasm of plants. Botanical gardens are an important part of the national and international effort to preserve seeds

At the Seed Savers Exchange Heritage Farm in Decorah, Iowa, thousands of heirloom vegetable varieties are grown from seed. Cages are used on these pepper plants to prevent cross-pollination.

and plants. A group of botanical gardens in North America has formed the Center for Plant Conservation. Each member-garden is responsible for maintaining a specific collection of plants for research and serves as a backup in the event a plant becomes extinct in the wild.

Additionally, a number of nonprofit organizations, concerned by the loss of heirloom seeds and traditional Native American crops, sprung up in the 1970s and '80s to help preserve and safeguard America's heritage of biodiversity. One of the first was Seed Savers Exchange, founded in 1975 by Kent and Diane Whealy (see "Seeds and Diversity: Edible Plants," page 22, written by Kent Whealy). Diane's grandfather had given the couple three kinds of heirloom seeds just before he died. Inspired by this act, the Whealys began seeking out other heirloom varieties and eventually joined with like-minded individuals to preserve historic vegetables, herbs, and flowers.

Today, Seed Savers has 8,000 members in North America and around the world, each of whom pays a small annual membership fee to be able to order seeds from other members. At Seed Savers' 140-acre farm in Decorah, Iowa, more than 18,000 heirloom vegetable varieties are grown organically; thousands more are grown throughout North America by Seeds Savers volunteers. In the last several years, the exchange has

Native Seeds/SEARCH in Tucson, Arizona, preserves and disseminates the seeds of traditional crops grown by Native Americans, such as pumpkins and squash.

expanded the scope of its operations to include finding and preserving heirloom cultivars from Russia and Eastern Europe. The 440-page 1997 Seed Savers Exchange "Yearbook" details the 19,467 vegetable varieties available to members; the fourth edition of the their invaluable *Garden Seed Inventory* provides gardeners with a list of more than 6,000 nonhybrid vegetables as well as the names of the commercial companies that sell them.

Native Seeds/SEARCH, based in Tucson, Arizona, was founded in 1983 to find, preserve, and disseminate seeds of traditional crops grown by Native Americans. The nonprofit organization's seed bank contains nearly 1,800 varieties—including large collections of corn, chiles, beans, and squash—many of which are endangered wild relatives of cultivated species or varieties that are not being systematically preserved elsewhere. Suzanne Nelson, the organization's seed curator, says that, unlike federal seed banks, organizations like Native Seeds/SEARCH promote the use of endangered crops as living entities.

There are still more organizations working to preserve our seed legacy. The Heirloom Seed Project, operated by the Landis Valley Museum in Lancaster, Pennsylvania, preserves plants grown in 18th- and 19th-century Pennsylvania German communities. The Thomas Jefferson Center for Historic Plants also maintains a collection of 18th- and 19th-century ornamental and edible plants. Smaller still are organizations like CORNS, a one-family operation in Turpin, Oklahoma, which preserves hundreds of corn cultivars, with names like 'Country Gentleman' and 'Howling Mob'.

In addition to governmental agencies and nonprofit organizations, an enthusiastic and growing group of commercial seed companies specializing in heirloom and open-pollinated cultivars has developed. Among the best known are Southern Exposure Seed Exchange in Earlysville, Virginia, which offers a gift certificate redeemable from their catalog in exchange for seeds of heirloom plants that are new to them. Seeds Blüm is Jan Blüm's company in Boise, Idaho, that specializes in open-pollinated vegetables with superb flavor. Garden City Seeds in Hamilton, Montana, focuses on heirloom and open-pollinated seeds for short growing seasons. (For the addresses of these and other seed companies, see "Seed Sources," page 92.)

SOCIETY SEED EXCHANGES

Another way both common and unusual seeds are preserved and spread is through plant and regional horticultural society seed exchanges. Many of these groups promote or facilitate formal and informal exchanges of seeds among their members. The North American Rock Garden Society sponsors a seed exchange, as do the American Horticultural Society, the American Hibiscus Society, the American Gourd Society, the American Primrose Society, the California Native Plant Society, the Cycad Society, the Hardy Plant Society of Oregon, the Herb Society of America, the Indoor Gardening Society of America, the Kansas and New England wildflower societies, the North American Fruit Explorers, the Rose Hybridizers Association, the Sedum Society, and the Species Iris Group of North America.

Specialist gardeners with exotic tastes may want to join the Botanical Society of South Africa, the British Pelargonium & Geranium Society, the Canadian Orchid Society, the International Clematis Society, or the Society for Growing Australian Plants. One of the best sources of information about plants societies is Barbara Barton's *Gardening by Mail* (see "For More Information," page 100).

The preservation of the genetic diversity of our food and ornamental plants—and the marvelous history and tradition that goes along with them—is something that we all can participate in. Ask older relatives or friends and you will likely find someone who grows an heirloom tomato or sweet pea. Try growing an heirloom yourself. It will give you the opportunity to watch, enjoy, and even taste, the slow workings of genetic adaptability.

GETTING STARTED WITH SEEDS

by Jennifer Bennett

GUNPOWDER AND BIBLES made history in the old West, but garden seeds made pioneering possible. In a letter Narcissa Prentice Whitman mailed from the nascent community of Vancouver, Washington, in 1836, she wrote: "We brought an assortment of seed from Cincinnati with us over the mountains. . . . When Brother Weld comes, please remember to fill his pockets with peaches, plums, and pear seeds, some of the best kind, and some good seed; what they have here is not of the best kind nor a great variety. Another very important article for us housewives, some broom corn seed."

Gardening life is much simpler now, at least when it comes to seeds of "the best kind" and "a great variety." You'll never be asked to fill your pockets with peach pits. But if obtaining seeds is easier than ever (see "Seed Sources," page 92), growing from seeds is much the same as it's always been, a process that still turns all of us into pioneers.

We adventurers have one thing going for us. A seed may have a low profile, but its entire business in life is to grow into a plant. The catch is that it doesn't want to waste its only shot by sprouting under the wrong circumstances. Giving it the go-ahead may be no more difficult than soak-

"One for the rook, one

for the crow;

One to die and

one to grow;

Plant your seeds

in a row,

One for the pheasant,

one for the crow,

One to eat and

one to grow."

TRADITIONAL RHYME

Beans have had a long working relationship with humanity and have become domesticated so that with enough warmth and water, they will obligingly sprout at any time of year.

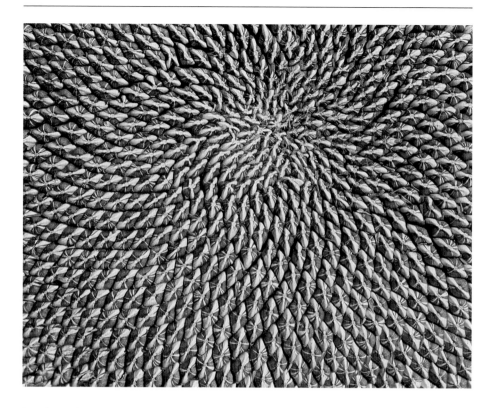

ing it and waiting for the root to pop out, much the way you do when you grow bean sprouts.

Beans are typical of the seeds that have had a long working relationship with humanity. They've become domesticated, the vegetable equivalent of a Holstein cow or a poodle. A domesticated seed, given enough warmth and water, will obligingly proffer a root pretty well any time of year. It's fortunate that the seeds people have grown for a long time are likely the ones you, too, will want to grow. Some of those seeds, such as apple seeds, take more coaxing: a number of hardy perennials, shrubs, and trees are downright fussy about sprouting. The cones of Rocky Mountain lodgepole pines (*Pinus contorta* var. *latifolia*), for instance, need the heat of a forest fire to open and free their seeds to germinate; seeds of Oregon-grape (*Mahonia aquifolium*) require four to six months of warm temperatures, then three to four months of cold to sprout. But when you grow common garden annuals, both flowers and vegetables, you're like a pioneer following a well-worn trail. Simply stay on the path and you'll end up with flowers and vegetables, just as your forebears did.

LEFT: Sunflower seeds, such as 'Mammoth Russian', can remain viable for up to seven years.

RIGHT: A seed of the sacred lotus sprouted after 1,200 years in storage.

BASIC REQUIREMENTS

To find the trail, you'll need a supply of quality seeds. Old seeds or seeds that have been improperly stored may be dead. Some seeds last for a very long time, but others need to be sown when fresh. Most members of the dill family (Umbelliferae), for instance, should be sown fresh every year. On the other hand, a seed of the sacred lotus (*Nelumbo nucifera*) germinated after 1,200 years in storage. Closer to home, basil seeds remain viable for at least five years if stored in a dry, cool location, and sunflowers for at least seven. If you're in doubt, buy or harvest a fresh supply, then store your leftovers properly (see "Collecting and Storing Seeds," page 80).

You'll also need to fulfill a few seed requisites. Many species don't need much, but even easy plants like beans have two requirements for sprouting: a suitable air temperature and a certain amount of moisture. Once germination takes place—unless your goal is crunchy sprouts for a sandwich—the seedlings will need containers holding soil or a similar porous medium in which the roots can grow. You can garden hydroponi-cally in nutrient-enriched water, but this chapter assumes you are

THIS IS A TEST

Although the seeds of many plants remain viable for several years, germination tends to decrease over time. If you're using old seeds, test them before planting by presprouting them on damp paper towels (see instructions for presprouting, page 63). If the germination rate is lower than 55 percent (divide the number of seeds that sprout by the number tested), buy new seeds. If the rate is between 55 and 85 percent, use the seeds but plant more thickly than the seed package recommends.

growing your seedlings for an eventual life in soil. Sooner or later, your plants will also need bright light and moisture.

TIMING IS (ALMOST) EVERYTHING

When should you sow your seeds? This depends upon three variables: the type of seeds, your climate, and when you want your flowers to bloom or your vegetables to mature.

Type of Seeds

Seeds vary greatly in the length of time they take to germinate. Given moisture and an optimum temperature range, some species, such as cress (*Lepidium sativum*), sprout in as few as two days; most garden seeds germinate in a week or two. If conditions are close to ideal and nothing has sprouted in a month, give up and start again. The longer the seeds take to germinate, the earlier you should be sowing them.

Different plants also take different lengths of time to mature, so you should pace your sowing accordingly.

Your Climate

The last spring frost and the first fall frost in your garden are benchmarks around which all planting dates are calculated. Plant growth slows or stops when temperatures drop to freezing. Furthermore, many plants are killed by frost, so they must be protected if their lifespan overlaps the frost dates. In spring, the customary means of protection is to start seeds indoors then transplant them outdoors when the weather is warm. Much later—around or after the frost-free date—the seeds of frost-tender plants

Once a gardener has planted self-sowing hardy annuals, such as these California poppies, they never have to be planted again.

may be sown outdoors. (See "A Time to Sow," below.) To find out the frost dates for your area, contact the local horticultural society, Extension Service, or weather bureau.

Timing the Bloom or Harvest

While late winter through early summer is the main seed-sowing time—and the time when the best selection of fresh seeds is available—some species can be sown any time of year. Certain hardy annuals, for instance, can go into your garden beds any time in winter or spring, though they won't germinate until the soil warms to their liking. Some of these flowers include Shirley, or field, poppy (*Papaver rhoeas*), California poppy (*Eschscholzia californica*), cosmos (*Cosmos bipinnatus*), and clary salvia (*Salvia viridis*). Once you grow these flowers, you may never have to sow them again. They drop their seeds in summer, and these seeds again wait until conditions suit them to germinate. Fewer vegetables self-sow, but you might want to stagger plantings of certain vegetable seeds to extend the harvest. In regions with cold winters, lettuce and radishes can be sown every two weeks from early spring until early summer, then again in autumn, to provide salads for many months.

A TIME TO SOW—INDOORS

These are suggested timings for indoor sowing of common plants. The number of weeks in the lists that follow refers to the time before the aver-

Carrot seeds can be sown directly outdoors five to seven weeks before the last frost, and after they flower, the seeds can be collected for the next season.

age date of the last spring frost in your area. For example, if your frost-free date is May 15, sow celery 12 weeks earlier, February 20. (Alternately, all of these plants can be seeded directly outdoors around or after the last frost date, although they will probably mature later.)

Ten to twelve weeks: celery, eggplant, leek, onion, pepper, eustoma (*Lisianthus*), impatiens, lobelia, pelargonium, verbena, and many perennial flowers

Seven to nine weeks: early lettuce, globe artichoke, parsley, ageratum, begonia, coleus, nicotiana, petunia, salpiglossis, and salvia

Five to six weeks: early cabbage, cauliflower, late celery, early leaf lettuce, and most small-seeded annual flowers

Four to five weeks: basil, cucumber, gourd, melon, pumpkin, squash, large-seeded annual flowers, and annual flowering vines

A TIME TO SOW—OUTDOORS

Five to seven weeks: broad bean, carrot, pea, spinach, turnip, onion sets, dill, parsley, alyssum, candytuft, pansy, poppy (*Papaver* and *Eschscholzia* species), black-eyed Susan (*Rudbeckia hirta*), clary salvia, snapdragon, annual stock, sunflower, sweet pea, and shrubs such as pea-tree (*Caragana*) and bush-clover (*Lespedeza*)

Three to four weeks: all in the list above; also beets, broccoli, Brussels

Sow the seeds of cabbage directly outdoors three to four weeks before the last frost, or plant early cabbage indoors five to six weeks before the last frost.

sprout, cabbage, collard, chard, kale, lettuce, potato eyes, radish, Canterbury-bells, clarkia (*Godetia grandiflora*), hollyhock, and mallow

Two to three weeks: All in lists above; also sweet corn, gladiolus and other summer bulbs, morning glory and other annual flowering vines.

Around the last spring frost: All of the above; also bean, peanut, cauliflower, cucumber, summer and winter squash, lavatera, marigold, and zinnia

One to two weeks after the last spring frost: All in the lists above; also lima bean, soybean, muskmelon, watermelon, sweet potato slips, basil, summer savory, sweet marjoram, and castor bean

TEMPORARY HOUSING

Unless you use soil blocks (see "Block Party," page 68), seeds sown indoors will need containers. Because these containers will be used for only a short time, they don't need to be deeper than two or three inches. However, they must allow water to drain out the bottom, and they should hold enough soil so the seedling will not be constantly drying out or instantly rootbound. Either give each seedling its own container, in which case the containers can be as small as an inch wide (the cells of the plastic four- or six-packs in which commercially grown seedlings are sold are fine, but the cells of an egg carton are not deep enough), or grow seedlings together in undivided containers or flats. Seeds can be sown fairly thickly, either in rows or in a cluster of several seeds, but once they germinate, they should be thinned so that each plant never touches its neighbor.

When starting seeds indoors, it is important to use clean containers and a light, porous, sterile soil mixture.

Plant pots, plastic dairy containers, plastic baked-goods containers, or cardboard milk cartons (either on their ends or on their sides, the top cut away, and the bottom perforated) all make suitable containers. Just make sure they are clean before you plant, and punch some holes in the bottom. Cover these holes with a single piece of newsprint to prevent soil from flowing out with the drainage water.

Absorbent or permeable containers, such as terra cotta or peat pots, are much more susceptible to drying out than plastic containers. Soak them before sowing, and afterwards, if necessary, keep them in a shallow bath of water to prevent drying, which will happen from the outside in. If a container has held soil in the past, it may be contaminated with fungal spores. Scrub previously used containers in a solution of one part household bleach to nine parts water.

SOIL

Soil for seeds sown indoors should be porous, lightweight, and sterile. All three demands can be met if you purchase a seed-starting mixture from a garden store (to make your own seed-starting medium, see "Make & Bake," opposite). Unlike commercial potting soils, which are too heavy for starting seedlings, these special mixes are a combination of ingredi-

MAKE & BAKE

A good medium for starting seeds can be made at home, but if any of the ingredients come from the garden, they should be sterilized before they are used in order to kill weed seeds and soil diseases, which may cause damping-off. If you want to use your own compost or garden soil, sterilize it by spreading it no more than 4 inches deep in a baking pan and covering it with foil; bake in the oven at 200° for 2 hours. Leave it in the containers to cool. Mix it with ⅓ vermiculite or perlite and ⅓ peat. To every 8 quarts of mixture, add 1 tablespoon of limestone.

The safest starting medium consists only of purchased, sterile ingredients, such as a mixture of ½ peat moss and ½ vermiculite or perlite to which a small amount of ground limestone is added (for example, 2 quarts of peat, 2 quarts of vermiculite, and 2 teaspoons of ground limestone).

ents, usually peat, vermiculite, and perlite, perhaps with the addition of limestone and wetting agents. Vermiculite and perlite are mineral products that expand with heat; they are lightweight, sterile, and will hold several times their weight in water. Soil for seeding need not include fertilizer, as seeds don't require nutrients to germinate, but many seedling mixtures do include fertilizer because the seedlings will require it later on.

Seed-starting mixtures may be damp when you first open the bag, but they will soon dry out. Before using them for seeding, pour the amount you need into a pail or large bowl and stir in enough warm water to make a doughy, wet mixture. Then pack the containers lightly to within ¼ inch of the rim so that when you water, it won't overflow. Water again before seeding.

SOME LIKE IT HOT

You may have noticed that certain weeds sprout outdoors early in spring, while others appear much later. That's because some seeds can germinate in soil as cold as 40°F, while others require a soil temperature of 55°, 60°, or higher. So it is with the seeds that you sow. If the temperature is right for them, they'll germinate relatively quickly. If temperatures are cooler than they like, germination will be slower. If the soil is too

CHAPTER VI

cold—or wet—the seeds may not sprout at all. Soil that is too hot can prevent germination also.

For most common plants sown indoors, a room temperature between 60° and 80° is fine for sprouting. The optimum temperature range for germination is often listed on the seed packet or in the seed catalog. Incidentally, this temperature is that of the soil medium, not necessarily the air, although the two are usually within a few degrees of each other.

If you keep your thermostat turned down or your flats on the floor, you may have to provide additional heat to germinate seeds. Heat is most efficiently used and most beneficial to the seeds and seedlings if it comes from below. There are electric seed-starting mats and cables on the market that provide a gentle bottom heat to containers placed on top, or you can set seeded containers over a mild heat source, such as the top of a refrigerator. Don't place your containers where their seeds or seedlings

Seeds can be sown fairly thickly (top), but once they germinate, they should be thinned so that each plant never touches its neighbor (bottom).

will bake—temperatures over 95°—and remember that bottom-heated soil dries out more quickly, so check daily to see if watering is necessary. Also stay away from the warm top of your furnace, as its fumes inhibit germination of many species.

GETTING A HEADSTART

Presprouting seeds, which is germinating seeds before they are planted, has two advantages. One, it means that you plant only viable seeds and thus won't waste good seeds by overplanting and then having to thin. Two, it means you can germinate your seeds in a warm place indoors even if you don't have room for a half-dozen flats or pots. For most households, an entire garden's worth of tomatoes, peppers, or tender flowers—some of the best candidates for this treatment—can be presprouted on a surface area not much bigger than a loaf of bread. Don't try to presprout tiny seeds, which are difficult to handle, and don't presprout seeds that dislike handling, such as cucumber and other members of the squash family.

To presprout seeds, you must keep them moist and warm. It is easiest to use a damp paper towel spread on the bottom of a covered container, such as a cottage cheese tub. Before you wet the towel, write the cultivar names on it in ballpoint pen. Press the towel into the container, dampen it with lukewarm water, sprinkle the seeds over it—about 25 percent more seeds than the number of plants you want, to make up for poor or slow germination—and cover the container. Put the container in a place that is warm but never hotter than 90°. Check the seeds every day, moistening the towel if necessary, then transplant the seeds to flats or other containers as soon as a tiny root emerges. The planted seedlings can stay in the same warm place until a green shoot shows above the soil surface; then they must be moved into bright light.

SOWING SEEDS

Indoors

Most seeds need darkness to germinate and must be covered with moist seedling mix, usually twice as deep as the thickness of the seed. To sow in flats, make furrows with a knife blade or with the edge of a ruler pressed into the soil; for individual containers, make an indentation with a pencil or your fingertip before setting the seed or a few seeds in place. Cover seeds lightly. Sow roughly twice as many seeds as the number of plants you want, since you will lose about half to nongermination, thinning, and transplanting. Seeds of a few plants, such as celery, dill, bellflower, coleus, nicotiana, and stock, germinate better in light than in darkness and should be scattered on an uncovered, moist soil surface rather than covered.

If the seeds are very fine, as those of ageratum, begonia, and petunia are, make sure the planting surface is damp, level, and lightly pressed before sowing. Sprinkle some seeds into the palm of your hand and wipe them as evenly as possible over the soil surface with the fingers of your other hand. Don't let the soil surface dry out—a spray bottle turned to its finest setting is good for daily misting. Set the containers in an area with diffused light, such as a few feet from a window or near but not under fluorescent lights.

There are a few species, such as primulas, whose seeds need darkness but don't want to be covered. Sprinkle these seeds on the surface of a dampened soil mix and press them down lightly. Then place the containers in a dark spot or cover them with pieces of cardboard or newsprint. Check under the covers daily. As soon as you see green shoots, remove the covers and move the containers into light.

If seeds have unusual germination needs, such as light or especially high or low temperatures, they will usually be described on the seed packet or in the seed catalogue. If nothing is said and the seeds are for familiar species, you can assume that they require the typical light covering of damp soil.

Outdoors

Seeds sown directly outdoors should also be kept moist until they germinate. Wet the ground and then make furrows or indentations. Sow about three times as many seeds as the number of plants you want, covering to the depth recommended on the packet, or about three times the diameter of the seed. Space small seeds like carrot about ⅛ inch apart, medium-sized seeds like beet about ½ inch apart, and large seeds like pea 1 or 2 inches apart. If you're sowing in a permanent location, create rows that are far enough apart to allow for easy weeding and walking. Seeds of plants that will become large, such as cabbage, broccoli, or cucumber, can be sown in stations, a few seeds together in a cluster that is eventually thinned to only one or two plants. Stations, or hills, are usually spaced a foot or two apart.

Check the seeded area every day, and water the surface with a fine spray if it dries out. In a very dry, windy climate, you may need to cover

Create rows that are far enough apart to allow for easy weeding and walking. A mulch of leaves for these tomatoes helps lower the evaporation rate of water from the soil and moderate its temperature.

areas sown with fine seeds, such as carrot, with boards or fabric to hold in moisture. Leave the covers in place for a few days, then check for signs of sprouting. As soon as green shoots appear, remove the covers but continue to water as needed.

MOISTURE

Moisture is necessary to trigger germination. It is important that the seed-starting mixture be uniformly damp before you plant into it. Flats and other containers can be placed in a saucer or pan of warmish water for constant bottom watering, although too much wetness encourages fungus diseases. Bottom watering works best with containers like terracotta or peat pots that dry out quickly. In other cases, it is better to use a fine mist to spray the soil surface whenever it begins to dry. Remember, finally, that the temperature of the water you use to water seeds—and the emerging seedlings—is just as important as soil temperature. Indoors, the water should be at least room temperature; outdoors, the water should be the ambient (air) temperature.

Some seeds will germinate more quickly if they receive special treatment. Here the hard outer shells of morning glory seeds are being nicked with a file.

SPECIAL HANDLING

The seeds of some species will germinate more quickly if given special treatment. Among the germination-speeding methods you may see recommended on seed packets and in garden books are:

Scarification

Some hard-shelled seeds, such as sweet pea and balloon vine, benefit from the outside coating being scratched or nicked to speed germination. One easy way to scarify seeds is to rub them lightly between two pieces of fine sandpaper. Abrade only the outer coating—you don't want to harm the embryo within.

Some seeds requiring scarification
Camellia species, Camellias
Cercis canadensis, Redbud
Cladrastis kentukea (*C. lutea*), Yellow-wood
Cornus florida, Flowering dogwood
Gleditisia triacanthos, Honey locust
Koelreuteria paniculata, Golden raintree
Paeonia suffruticosa, Tree peony
Rosa blanda, Meadow rose

Soaking

The germination of some seeds can be speeded up if they are soaked in lukewarm water for several hours before planting. It is important to plant

DAMPING-OFF

Damping-off, also called seedling blight, is a collective name for several strains of fungus that attack seedlings either underground or at the soil surface, toppling them at the base. It is most common in warm, damp conditions. The best preventatives are clean pots and tools and a sterile soil mix (especially those containing peat), although occasionally damping-off is introduced through water or dirty seeds. Excessive watering and fertilizing also encourage outbreaks of damping-off.

If you see seedlings that look pinched at the base and have fallen over, you may still be able to save any remaining healthy seedlings in the same container. Transplant all the healthy seedlings into clean containers filled with fresh, sterilized soil mix. Discard the remaining infected soil and all infected seedlings.

these seeds immediately after soaking and to water them thoroughly after planting. They must not be allowed to dry out again before germination occurs.

Some seeds requiring soaking
Abelmoschus esculentus, Okra
Albizia julibrissin, Mimosa or silk tree
Armeria species, Thrift
Cytisus species, Brooms
Helianthus species, Sunflowers
Ipomoea species, Morning glories
Lupinus species, Lupines
Pastinaca sativa, Parsnip
Pisum sativum, Pea
Wisteria species, Wisterias

Stratification

The seeds of many plants that are native to regions with cold winters require a period of moist coolness before they will germinate. This process of applying moist cold, called stratification, can be mimicked indoors and need not take all winter. Three to five weeks are usually suffi-

BLOCK PARTY

Soil blocks are cubes of planting mix compressed in special molds, or blockers, which are made of metal or plastic and sold by garden stores and catalogs. Soil blocks have the advantage of needing no containers. Moreover, plant roots are "air pruned" when they reach the edge of the block, forming a compact root ball. Transplanting is as easy as popping the cube into the ground. On the negative side, soil blocks can be messy to handle, sometimes crumble, and are difficult to label individually.

Each standard-sized block, which is about 2 inches cubed, is meant to hold one seedling. (Also available are soil blockers that make tiny ¾-inch cubes, meant to hold a seed only until it germinates, and much larger blockers, which permit "potting up"). If you sow more than one seed in the block, thin to the healthiest seedling. As the seedling grows, its roots help bind the block, increasing its strength. Slow-growing seedlings can spend their entire indoor lives in soil blocks, while fast-growing seedlings can be transplanted, soil block and all, into a larger block or into a container before planting outdoors.

The mix used for making soil blocks must be high in organic matter, which acts as a binder. You can purchase commercial soil-block mixes or make your own. The standard recipe calls for 4 parts sphagnum peat, 2 parts aged and sifted compost, and 2 parts coarse sand or perlite, to which small amounts of lime and kelp meal are added. Instructions for making mixes and soil blocks are included when you purchase a blocker.

cient, and the temperature in a refrigerator, just above freezing, does the job. Mix the seeds with damp peat moss and place in a small, labelled plastic bag tied with a twist tie, or a sealed glass jar. When rootlets appear inside the bag or jar, take it out of the refrigerator and plant the seeds in pots. Place the containers under grow lights or in a cool, bright window.

Seeds can also be stratified outdoors, either by sowing them directly into garden beds or in plastic pots in the fall. Pots should be overwintered against a north-facing house wall or in a cold frame—some place that offers protection against full sun and wind. Set the pots into a bed of straw, fallen leaves, or grass clippings, which will insulate them and allow drainage. Water if their soil becomes dry.

Some seeds requiring stratification
Acer species, Maples (except red maple [*A. rubrum*] and silver maple
    [*A. saccharinum*])
Aesculus species, Buckeyes, horse-chestnuts
Amelanchier species, Shadbushes, serviceberries
Cornus species, Dogwoods
Iris species, Irises
Magnolia species, Magnolias
Pinus species, Pines
Rosa species, Species roses
Thalictrum species, Meadow rues
Vitis species, Grapes
(For more seeds that require stratification, see page 35.)

Inoculation

Seeds of the bean, or pea, family (Leguminosae) may germinate and grow better if they are inoculated with certain strains of soil bacteria. In many cases, these bacteria are naturally present in the soil, especially if the plant or a relative has grown there before. Otherwise, inoculants can be purchased from suppliers of farm and vegetable seeds. The inoculant is a powder that is mixed with the seeds just before they are sown. Inoculation is usually done only when it's important that the harvest be as large as possible; for instance, in the commercial growing of soybeans. (Don't confuse seeds that have been inoculated with *Rhizobium* bacteria with seeds that have been treated with Captan or other toxic pesticides. Avoid seeds that have been doused with chemicals; seed catalogs that offer treated seeds usually offer untreated seeds as well.)   🌀

CARING FOR SEEDLINGS

by Shepherd Ogden

IT'S OVERCAST AND light drizzle falls. Frost is done for this season, and temperatures are in the 60s. The soil is dark and crumbly, firm but not packed. The trays of seedlings have been hardened-off. You take one of those stocky plants, knock the plant gently from its pot, and admire the fibrous root ball. You sweep aside a handful of soil, set the plant in the moist earth, and with both hands, pull a bit of soil back around the base of the plant, pressing down firmly. Ahh, to dream.

More often, the sun is merciless, the wind and rain icy cold. Pests and diseases lie waiting. The plants themselves are stressed, too big for their pots, long and spindly. Fortunately, there are things you can do to ensure that your seedlings have a real shot at success, even when conditions are not ideal.

THE INDOOR SEASON

Each seed is made up of a tiny genetic model of its parent and a supply of food. This package is dried for storage, but as soon as conditions and genetics permit, it springs back to life. After a few hours (or days, depending on the species), the first seedling root, called the radicle, emerges. As the radicle grows, the seed's starch and sugar reserves are sent to the growing tip, and tiny feeder roots begin to spread throughout the soil. Soon the plant breaks ground and finds the last growth factor it needs: light. A new plant is on its way.

If you didn't add fertilizer to the seed-starting mix, you'll need to start both watering and fertilizing after the seedling develops its first true leaves. From this point on, the new plant is dependent on the nutrients its roots can find in the soil, the moisture that makes them available, and the quality of light its leaves receive. Without the right amount of each—in proper proportion to each other and the temperature—no plant will thrive.

Since both heat and light fuel plant growth, the relationship between the two is critical. A common mistake among home gardeners is to keep plants at too high a temperature for the amount of light they receive. What often happens is that the gardener tries to compensate for

Transplants should be held by the root ball and planted equally distant in well-prepared soil. These celeriac seedlings are being planted in a chipped-leaf mulch.

BABY FOOD

The feeding mix I used when I was growing bedding plants to sell—and for my own garden—was 1 tablespoon each of liquid fish fertilizer (or fish emulsion) and liquid seaweed per gallon of water. This is the full-strength formula and should be diluted 4 to 1 if you fertilize seedlings every time you water.

slow growth with more fertilizer and higher temperatures. The result is limp, leggy seedlings that are hard-put to cope with outdoor conditions when planting time arrives.

On cloudy days, the experienced gardener lowers the temperature to compensate for the lower light levels. While every plant has a temperature range it likes best, within that range, the cooler you keep the temperature, the better off the plant will be. Don't take things too far, though. A combination of low temperature, low light, and overwatering is ideal for the development of the damping-off fungus (for more information, see "Damping-off," page 67). For most common flower and vegetable seedlings, temperatures between 60° and 70° F are about right.

Seedlings also need plenty of light. Not only is the light from a south-facing window more short-lived than it might seem (rarely exceeding eight hours a day), but the glass in house windows screens out some parts of the sunlight that plants need. For the best growth, use fluorescent lights—set four or five inches above the plants' foliage—and keep them on for at least 14 hours a day.

Fertilizer and water also need to be kept in proper proportion. Plants need nutrients to grow, and without enough moisture they will not only be unable to take up those nutrients, they will wilt and die. However, it is important to remember that too much water washes away the nutrients in the tray or pot, and the plants will starve. The conventional wisdom holds that you should feed young plants every seven to 10 days, but this is not accurate. Rather, feeding should correspond to the number of waterings. One solution is to fertilize each time you water, at ¼ strength. That way you don't need to keep track of when you last fertilized, and the plants get an even, constant supply of nutrients.

Keep an eye out for signs of over- or under-fertilization. Leaves that curl under are a sign of overfeeding, whereas discoloration is usually a

Seedlings, such as this white kale, need plenty of light and the right amount of moisture and nutrients.

sign of underfeeding. If the plant is pale, it is likely deficient in nitrogen. Leaves with purplish undersides indicate a shortage of phosphorus; leaves with bronze edges a shortage of potassium. Since seaweed and fish fertilizers contain balanced amounts of all these nutrients, the solution is simply to increase or decrease the strength or frequency of feedings.

MOVING OUTDOORS

It's not enough to raise healthy seedlings if they are so pampered that they can't survive the sun, wind, rain, and seesaw effect of day and night temperature changes. I can get brisk sunny days in the 60s in spring, only to have the temperature fall into the 30s after sunset. But frosty nights aren't the only enemy of tender transplants. Wind can be just as hard on young plants, snapping off brittle stems or flattening them to the ground where they can fall prey to diseases and insects. Even the sun on which they are so dependent can be dangerous: plants grown indoors develop extra photosynthetic cells in the leaves. A sudden increase in light can cause them to overload, then shrivel and fall.

All of these problems are solved by hardening-off, or acclimating, seedlings. At first, move your plants outside for a few hours in the afternoon; then gradually increase the time they spend in the open air, exposed to the sun and wind. Hardening-off is one of the best uses of a cold frame, a low, bottomless structure that looks like a miniature greenhouse, with a transparent top that can be opened for ventilation. Keep the frame closed (or open slightly) for the first few days, then open it completely for longer and longer periods each day until your plants are ready to be planted in the garden.

Preparing the Garden

To get the garden ready for transplants, I use a spading fork to turn and open the soil. (I also use a board to stand on, which reduces soil compaction.) Next, I rake the surface to remove any rocks or stubble and break up any clods. If I'm working in a flower border, setting out a single plant or a couple of plants, the process is the same. I turn and open the soil with a spading fork, making sure to remove any debris or clods that might interfere with the transplants' root development.

If your soil is well prepared—rich in organic matter—making a transplant hole is no more than a poke of the finger. For larger plants, a quick scoop with the hand is all it takes. If your garden soil is rich and healthy, no additional fertilizer is necessary at planting time; if your soil isn't in top-notch shape and does not have sufficient nutrients, you may want to add compost to each planting hole or row.

If your plants show symptoms of nutrient deficiency (see above), side-dress or apply alongside them an organically stable fertilizer that they can take in immediately, such as fish emulsion.

Transplanting

The process of setting plants outdoors is fairly straightforward. In the vegetable garden, I like to plant in beds, setting the seedlings equally distant from one another in a hexagonal pattern. Once the plants grow to full size, their leaves will cover the entire surface of the bed. This arrangement reduces the plants' competition with weeds and makes the best use of the space available. If you're setting out perennial transplants—species that will remain in the same spot for many years—be sure that you've loosened the soil to a good depth and width and enrich it with organic matter, such as compost.

When I work with transplants, I always hold them by the root ball or by the leaves, never the stem. Healthy tops can grow new roots, and a good root system can replace damaged or missing leaves, but the stem is the bridge between the two. Hurt it and the plant has no way to move its nutrients and water.

I loosen the roots a bit if they're especially tangled, then place them firmly into a planting hole at the same level, or very slightly deeper, than they were in the container. A few species—tomatoes are one example—can be planted much deeper than they were growing: The buried stem will sprout new roots.

If plants have thick, fleshy roots, spread the roots and place them in a hole that is large enough so they don't need to be doubled over. Sift soil

A cold frame gives tender seedlings some protection from the elements while helping them acclimate to outdoor conditions.

in around the roots to make sure that no air is trapped underneath, and water well. If the top of the plant is large, stake it so the wind can't pull at the roots before they reset their anchor.

Fibrous-rooted plants that have filled a pot and made a tight ball of soil and roots can't really be loosened. I've found that kneading a fibrous root ball rips out a small percentage of the tiny root hairs and gets them to start growing again. It's like shaking a friend to wake him or her from a bad dream: You can't be too gentle or you won't get anywhere.

Sun

Garden plants live on sun. But too much is almost as bad for plants as it is for people. When you move plants outside, they get double or triple the light they're used to. That's why hardening-off transplants is so important: it gets them used to all the conditions of the open garden.

Wait for an overcast day to set your seedlings in the garden; if you have to transplant on a sunny day, wait until late afternoon, when the strength of the sun has mellowed. That gives the plants overnight to adjust. If the following day is going to be sunny too, give your plants some shade until they get established.

One way to provide shade is to put the seedlings in a box or basket, but make sure there are plenty of holes to let in light and air. Even a couple of evergreen boughs will provide welcome respite from the sun. You can shade large numbers of plants with salvaged window screens

A NON (HEAD) STARTER

Keep in mind that, all else being equal, you are better off with young, vigorous plants than older, root-bound ones. The best flowers and vegetables come from plants that grow quickly, without what the pros call "checks," shortages of any nutrient, water, or temperatures to their liking. If the plants are a little small when it's time to plant outdoors, all you've lost is a week or two in the garden, and that is often made up in the good growing days of early summer. Two weeks in March is only worth a couple of days in May, or so we say in the nursery trade.

propped up on blocks over the row or bed. A high-tech and more expensive alternative is to put up tunnels using polypropylene shade cloth supported by wire hoops.

Water

Whether it's sunny or cloudy, water in transplants well. If you can get a hose into the garden there is a great way to get plants off to a good start: Take a hose with a trigger-grip nozzle down the row, aim the nozzle at each spot where a plant will be set, and pull the trigger for a second. The blast of water will create a small hole full of soil soup into which the waiting plant can be dropped. Pull dry soil from the surrounding bed loosely over the moist area, leaving the transplant at the same depth it had been in its container.

You can also mulch transplants to help lower the evaporation rate of water from the soil and temper its climate. In warm or hot regions, use a thick cover of organic matter that is free of weed seeds; in cool climates, clear or black plastic is preferable because it helps retain moisture while letting the sun warm the soil. Water thoroughly or wait for rain before applying plastic mulches or you'll have a mini-desert under the mulch.

During a drought, water your plants in the evening so that evaporation won't steal the water before it has a chance to soak into the soil. Second best is very early morning, before sunrise. If you don't have a mulch, cultivate lightly as soon as the surface of the soil is dry. This breaks the capillary action of the soil and prevents moisture from wicking to the surface, where it can be drawn off by the wind.

In warm or hot regions, mulch new plants in spring using a thick cover of organic matter that is free of weed seeds, such as partially composted leaves.

Wind

Wind can be even more stressful than sun, as wind drastically increases the flow of water through the plant. The roots draw water from the soil, which travels up through the stem to the leaves, where most of it transpires into the air. This movement of water is essential to the plant, because the pressure of its passage helps hold the leaves upright and open to the sun and because, without enough water, photosynthesis—the chemical conversion on which the plant is entirely dependent for its growth—grinds to a halt. When a seedling is set out in the garden, the tops are usually capable of moving a lot more water than the roots can supply. That's why you want to be careful not to disturb the roots—every little bit of extra water capacity helps.

If your newly set plants start to wilt and watering doesn't help, you can cut off up to a third of the top of the plant. That puts the plant back into balance by reducing the amount of leaf surface that is demanding water. The leaves will grow back, and the plant will be better off without the wilted leaves, which offer a spot for diseases to get established. As long as the plant's roots are healthy and the stem undamaged, the plant will recover quickly, and new leaves will grow.

The same shade covers that protect the plants from the sun will also keep the wind at bay; if the plant is too tall for a basket or a tunnel, put up a wind screen.

I once had to move a whole bed of large foxglove plants. I kept a shovelful of soil with each plant and after putting them in their new home, watered them in well. Then I put up a wind screen on the north and west sides of the bed. It was a relatively simple affair—commercial shade cloth stapled to 6-foot bean poles—but it kept the plants from being exposed to the full force of the wind. My wind screen worked beautifully—of more than a hundred plants, I didn't lose a single one.

Cold

Frost is the major concern of most gardeners when they set out their plants each spring. The last-frost date for any area is an average of many years, but you can't go by only the calendar when it comes to frost. Experienced gardeners use local signs—the blooming of certain plants or the appearance of particular migratory birds—to determine when the time is right to plant each crop.

The same devices that shelter your plants from too much sun and wind will give some protection from frost, with one difference. The more porous the cover—which is important for both sun and wind protection because of the need for ventilation—the less effective it will be against frost. The traditional fall frost protectors, such as blankets and sheets, don't work well for seedlings because their weight can damage the seedlings. Metal and glass, which conduct cold, are less effective than wood, plastic, and fiber covers.

There are many kinds of row covers and cloches available for frost protection, but if they are transparent they are likely to overheat on warm, sunny days. The best, in my opinion, are the spun-bonded floating row covers. These translucent white covers are so light they don't need any supports to keep from weighing down the plants, yet they provide 3° to 5°F of frost protection. In my garden, they have protected squash seedlings down to 28°F. Since they are relatively porous, they allow rain to pass through.

Pests

Even if your transplants survive the vicissitudes of the weather, there are still creatures that would love to make a meal of them Fortunately, there are effective ways to deal with these nightmares.

Take cabbage root maggots, for example. The pesticide typically recommended is Diazinon, but I won't use it. In the first few years of market gardening, I tossed a handful of wood ash around the base of each transplant. It worked but was too time consuming. Paper collars worked, too, but without the benefits of the potassium in the wood ash.

Then I read that the cabbage fly lays its eggs only until May 15 in my

READY OR NOT

Before you begin planting, test to be sure the soil is ready. Pick up a loose handful of soil, then close your hand and slowly squeeze it into a fist. No water should come out between your fingers. Unclench your fist. The clod of soil on your palm should be moist enough to hold together but not slick or shiny; the wrinkle and print lines of your hand should not be visible. Poke the clod with a twig. If it breaks apart into smaller clods, it is soil that's ready for spring planting.

part of the world. Sure enough, timing the crop so that I didn't transplant until after the fly was finished cut losses and our labor. Like timing for last frost, this is not a solid date, and asking experienced gardeners in your own area will give you an idea of how changing your garden schedule might make pest control a lot less trouble.

I also discovered that insects couldn't get under floating row covers if I sealed the edges with soil. Now, when I transplant, I cover the plants immediately with a floating row cover. The milky white color and grainy texture of the covers gives seedlings in the cabbage or mustard family respite from sun and wind, protects them from frost, and is 100 percent effective against cabbage root maggots. Better still, row covers protect against a host of other pests, making pesticides unnecessary.

Diseases

Diseases have diverse causes and symptoms. Many are already in your garden soil; others are brought in on seeds and transplants. The best cure is prevention: Buy seeds from reputable dealers or save your own, plant disease-resistant cultivars, and examine transplants carefully.

Healthy, vigorous transplants are less likely to be infected than spindly, weak ones. Make sure your plants aren't stressed—that they have the right amounts of light, water, and nutrients—by protecting them from temperature extremes and making sure they have adequate air circulation. Practice good sanitation in the garden: don't work around plants when they are wet, remove and burn any dead or diseased plants, and practice crop rotation.

COLLECTING & STORING SEEDS

by Suzanne Ashworth

WE AMERICANS HAVE access to the greatest number of plants ever, yet many species and cultivars are in danger of being lost for all time. Seed collecting in your own yard or in wild places is one way to increase even more the number of plants available to you. Saving and sharing seeds also helps forestall or prevent extinction of heirloom, uniquely adapted, or environmentally threatened plants. In addition, growing from seed provides gardeners personal satisfaction—and the admiration of those with whom they share their bounty.

Before racing outdoors, paper bag or bucket in hand, you should be aware of the basics of successful—and responsible—seed collecting. To start, take seeds from as many different individuals of the same species as possible, which increases the genetic diversity and health of the next generation of plants. Never take all of the seeds from any one plant when collecting in the wild. Leave plenty of seeds behind to ensure that the plants will be around next year.

Always check plants before collecting their seeds. Are they the correct color, size, and shape; did they grow well in your climate? Don't col-

He who sows thickly,

gathers thinly.

He who sows thinly,

gathers thickly.

TRADITIONAL WISDOM

Take seeds from as many individual plants as possible to increase the genetic diversity and health of the next generation.

LEFT: It's easy to hand-harvest seed, such as those of lettuce, using just about any clean and dry container.

lect seeds from plants that appear to be undersized, misformed, diseased, or particularly prone to insects. And unless you want to experiment, don't collect seeds from hybrid cultivars, as they will not "come true" when planted.

Labeling and photographing is an integral part of seed collecting. Nothing is more frustrating than ending up with several bags of mystery seeds. Label everything during each step of seed saving: the photographs, collection containers, drying trays, fermenting bowls, and storage containers. It's much easier to label than to discover that the flat of fennel you've been babying for two months is not fennel but Queen Anne's lace.

Seed collecting requires containers, and a myriad of ancient and modern containers are available. Dry seed pods and heads from such plants as beans and morning glory are easily collected in baskets. Check the weave to ensure that it is tight enough to prevent the seed from falling through the basket (many Native American basket designs are specially made for harvesting seeds). Baskets allow for good air circulation so that the seeds remain dry, and insect damage and rot are easy to spot, as the contents of a basket are visible.

Paper and cloth bags are often used for collecting dry seeds, especially when a large part of a plant is collected. Carrot umbels, zinnia heads, and pine cones are good candidates for bags. If you reuse bags, be sure that seeds from previous collecting haven't been left behind to contaminate the new harvest.

Fruits, berries, and other wet seeds are best collected in plastic buckets, tubs, and bowls. After processing, the seeds may be fermented or washed in the same containers. If you use containers from the kitchen, always thoroughly clean and sterilize them with a bleach solution (2 tablespoons of bleach to 1 quart of water) before again using them for food.

COLLECTING & PROCESSING DRY SEEDS

The seeds of nonfruit-bearing plants are usually harvested dry. Most flower heads as well as many vegetables, herbs, trees, shrubs, and vines produce seeds in pods that dry naturally where they stand. It is important to wait to collect seeds until the pods are nearly or fully dry (green plants that are pulled and dried produce little viable seed). In most flowers and vegetables, the ripest seed pods will be located at the bottom of

Before collecting seeds, always check plants, such as these parsnips, to make sure that they are growing well in your climate.

the stalk and should be hand-harvested as soon as they dry and darken in color; then continue to collect seeds as they mature. If hand-harvesting is too time consuming, cut the entire stalk when the greatest number of seed pods are dry but have not yet shattered, or broken open.

In most cases, dry pods are harvested individually into bowls or baskets. The seed pods are then rubbed, beaten, or flailed until the seeds fall free from the pods. While commercial seed firms use machines to harvest, thresh, and winnow seed crops, home gardeners must choose from other options. The most popular method is to place the pods in a cloth sack or pillow case and flail or tramp on it. Mashing pods between two boards works well with smaller seeds. Rubbing the seeds over a screen is best for seeds that are not completely enclosed in a pod, such as lettuce. Always exercise caution; really vigorous mashing or rubbing can break or split seeds.

Winnowing separates the debris and chaff from the seeds. Pictures of people tossing seeds out of baskets while the wind does the separating, make the process look quite appealing. In reality the wind is usually variable: It's easy to lose half your seeds when a gust passes by. And as the wind changes direction, it's also easy to end up covered with dust and chaff. Hair dryers and household fans are good wind substitutes. No matter what the winnowing method, the area should be covered. This way

The entire stalk of plants like broccoli can be cut and cleaned when the seed pods are dry but have not yet shattered.

seeds that are accidentally blown away with the chaff can be recovered.

When the seeds and chaff are of nearly the same weight, it's next to impossible to winnow the seeds successfully. Screening—seeds are passed through a screen that is just large enough for the seeds but which excludes larger pieces of chaff—is a good alternative. After screening, both seeds and very small chaff remain. The seeds are then screened again, using a screen that is smaller than the seeds this time. This process, which is called reverse screening—separates the seeds from most of the remaining chaff.

COLLECTING & PROCESSING WET SEEDS

Juicy pods and seeded fruits, such as tomatoes, passionflower, guava, elderberries, and wild solanums, fall off the plant naturally, decay slowly, and deposit their seeds on the surface of the earth. Collecting seeds from these plants is easy, for most seeds mature and are ready for saving as soon as the pods or fruits have changed color and are soft to the touch. Cutting the fruit open, scraping the seeds out, rinsing briefly under running water, and letting the seeds dry is often all the processing that is necessary.

The seeds of some plants, such as eggplant, are more difficult to separate from the flesh. To harvest, begin by cutting the fruits in half. Pull as much flesh as possible away from the seeded areas, and then mash the seeded flesh, either by hand or in a food processor. Place the mashed fruit in a bowl, add water, and let the seeds settle. Pour off the water and debris. Repeat the process several times. After the seeds are relatively free of flesh, add water a final time and strain the mixture. Place the seeds on a piece of glass or waxed paper (do not use paper for drying, as the seeds will stick to the paper and are nearly impossible to remove). Spread the seeds evenly over the surface and allow them to dry, stirring twice daily to ensure even drying and help prevent the seeds from clumping together.

The seeds of other plants, such as the tomato, must ferment before they are stored. Fermentation removes the chemical inhibitors that encase seeds and prevent germination inside the fruit. Artificial fruit fermentation mimics the natural rotting of the fruits and has the added bonus of killing some seed-borne diseases.

To process, mash or puree the fruits and place the seed mixture in a bowl. Add about half as much water as juice and seeds from the fruit and stir the mixture twice a day for about three days. Keep an eye out as the fermentation will proceed more quickly in warm temperatures. The bowl of seeds will become covered with white or gray mold during fermentation, so set it where it can't be accidentally tipped over and where you will not be able to smell it. When bubbles begin to rise to the top of the mass or when a good mold coat has formed, the fermentation should be stopped. If the process is allowed to continue too long, the seeds will begin to germinate.

After fermentation, add twice the amount of water as there are seeds and debris and stir the mixture. The good seeds will settle to the bottom of the bowl. Gently pour off the debris. Add more water and repeat the process until only seeds remain. Strain the seeds and spread them on a glass or ceramic surface to dry. Stir seeds twice a day to ensure even drying and prevent the seeds from clumping together. Some seeds will begin to germinate if they are not dried quickly, but don't be tempted to speed the process by moving them into direct sunlight or drying them in an oven. In hot, humid weather, a fan will help speed drying.

STORING SEEDS

Once seeds are cleaned and thoroughly dried, they need to be properly stored to ensure maximum viability. Many containers are available. A good choice is glass jars with rubber seals, such as baby food or canning jars. Plastic bags, tightly sealed and stored inside a large jar, also protect

To save tomato seeds, first squeeze or mash the fruits (upper left). Place the seed mixture in a bowl with half as much water. Stir it twice a day for about three days and allow it to ferment, which removes chemical inhibitors that prevent germination. When a good mold coat has formed (upper right), stop the fermentation by adding twice the amount of water and stirring. The seeds will settle to the bottom. Pour off the water and debris and repeat until only seeds remain. Wash the seeds clean in a strainer (left) and spread them on a glass or ceramic surface to dry.

seeds' viability. Once sealed in a container, seeds should be stored in a cool, dark location.

If you are collecting seeds on a regular basis, either annually or every two or three years, most seeds you save will remain viable. Germination

PLAYING MOTHER NATURE

Typically, plants produce both male and female flowers. Insects pick up pollen from the male flowers and deposit it on the female flowers. Insects, however, are not particular about the flowers they visit and randomly move pollen from flower to flower to flower. Many plants accept pollen from all cultivars within the same species, so their seeds may produce offspring that bear little resemblance to themselves. To avoid such cross-breeding—and to guarantee that the seeds you save will produce plants like their parents—you must prevent insects from visiting the flowers of plants you've selected for seed saving. Then you must perform the insects' job yourself.

The squash family, or Cucurbitaceae, is typical of plants requiring hand-pollination when more than one cultivar within a species is grown in close proximity. Squash is used here to exemplify the process of hand-pollination, but the techniques can be adapted for many other food and flower crops.

Hand-pollination should begin as soon as the plants start producing flowers. Each species of the squash family has slightly different characteristics, but all species set, or produce, only a limited number of fruits. Although plants will keep forming flowers, these will be aborted or dropped unless the existing fruits are damaged or removed. If the plants have already set numerous fruits that were insect-pollinated, remove them before hand-pollinating new flowers.

When hand-pollinating, use a male flower from one plant to pollinate a female flower on a different plant of the same cultivar. This technique, known as sibing, increases genetic diversity. When certain plant characteristics are desired, selfing is used. Selfing occurs

rates decline slightly over time, but the vast majority of seeds can be kept at least three years. You can also use a technique—freezing—to increase seeds' viability up to five times longer than their average rate.

For long-term storage, seeds must first be dried to a 6 to 8 percent moisture content. Color-indicating silica gel is used as a moisture desiccant, or absorber. The silica gel, which has been treated with cobalt chloride, looks like little plastic beads. The beads are deep blue when dry; as

Cages prevent cross-pollination by keeping insects from visiting the flowers of plants selected for seed saving.

when a female flower is pollinated using a male flower from the same plant.

Begin by distinguishing between the male and female flowers. In the Cucurbitaceae, a female blossom is attached to a small, visible fruit; a male blossom is attached to a straight stem. This is most obvious in squash blooms; melons, which have much smaller flowers, are more difficult to sex.

Blossoms that are ready to open are easy to identify: Regardless of their size, they will have begun to show color and their petals will have begun to flare. Select male and female flowers that will open in

Continues on page 90

they pick up moisture, they turn light pink. Silica gel can be reused by drying the beads in a 200°F oven. Once they are dry and bright blue, they are ready to be reused.

To begin the drying, label each seed sample and place it in a small paper packet. Weigh the seed packets and measure out the same weight of silica gel. Place the packets and silica gel in a jar and tightly seal the jar. After a week, the seed-moisture content should be reduced to the

the next 12 to 14 hours; then use masking tape to keep each blossom shut, noting whether it is male or female. (Flowers also can be protected from insects with paper, cloth, or net bags, floating row covers, and other barriers.) If the flowers are easily hidden by foliage, you may want to use stakes to mark the ones you've taped.

To complete the hand-pollination process, pick the male flower, remove the tape, and carefully tear off the flower's petals. Next, gently remove the tape from the female flower. The flower will open slowly. When untaping flowers be sure to work quickly, as bees have been known to race to flowers moments after they are open.

Take the male flower and gently rub the pollen onto the stigma of the female flower. Pollination will be more successful if several male flowers are used to pollinate each female flower. After pollinating the female flower, retape it shut. And to ensure you save the right seeds

ideal six to eight percent. Open the jar and remove the silica gel. Reseal the jar and store it in the freezer section of your refrigerator (if this is not possible, place the containers in a refrigerator or in a dry, cold area where the temperature fluctuates as little as possible).

When it's time to retrieve seeds from frozen storage, allow the jar to

To hand-pollinate a squash or other blossom, select a male and female flower and tape them shut (left). The next morning, remove the tape and gently rub pollen from the male flower onto the stigma of the female flower (right).

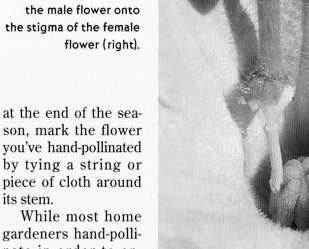

at the end of the season, mark the flower you've hand-pollinated by tying a string or piece of cloth around its stem. While most home gardeners hand-pollinate in order to ensure that the seeds of established cultivars they collect will come true, you may want to try to create a new cultivar. The technique is the same—but keep in mind that the plants you work with need to be closely related. You can't cross a tomato with a pepper, but you can pollinate a 'Stupice' tomato with a 'Brandywine'. Over time, your work could produce a fruit as cold-hardy as 'Stupice' but as flavorful as 'Brandywine'.

reach room temperature before opening it. If the jar is opened before the seeds reach room temperature, moisture will condense on the cold seeds and rehydrate them. Finally, since germination rates decline over time, you may want to test your seeds before planting them. For directions on how to test, or proof, seeds, see "This Is a Test," page 56.

SEED SOURCES

Y ou won't find seeds for the infamous 'Rat Turd' pepper on the rack at your local garden center, nor will you find seeds for 'Jenny Lind' melon or 'Greengage' tomato, two 19th-century cultivars. You won't find seeds for the flowering dogwood (*Cornus florida*), mushroom spawn, or more than one or two sweet pea cultivars. To get your hands on these treasures, you have to mine seed catalogs. Mail-order seed companies and organizations are as varied as the seeds they sell. There's everything from The Fragrant Path, a one-man show, to giants like Thompson & Morgan and W. Atlee Burpee & Co., which have scores of employees and thousands of customers.

The list that follows includes many of the best North American mail-order seed companies, both large, established firms and small, specialized, and regional companies. Also included are nonprofit organizations dedicated to preserving old and endangered cultivars and species. For even more seed sellers and sources, consult the new edition of *Gardening by Mail* (see page 100).

THE ABUNDANT LIFE
SEED FOUNDATION
P.O. Box 772
Port Townsend, WA
98368
(360) 385-5660
email: abundant@
olypen.com
Nonprofit; vegetables, grains, herbs, flowers, and woody plants, mostly heirlooms. Catalog $2.

AIMERS SEEDS
R.R. 3
Ilderton, ON
N0M 2A0 Canada
(519) 461-0011
1,500 flowers, trees, and shrubs. Catalog $4.

ALLEN, STERLING &
LOTHROP
191 U.S. Route 1
Falmouth, ME 04105
(207) 781-4142
Vegetables, herbs, and flowers, both old and new cultivars. Catalog $1, refundable with order.

ARROWHEAD ALPINES
P.O. Box 857
Fowlerville, MI 48836
(517) 223-3581
Hard-to-find seeds for 6,000 perennials, wildflowers, grasses, alpines, shrubs, vines, dwarf conifers, and trees. As of this writing, no seed list is available. Plant catalog $2.

AZTEKAKTI
11306 Gateway East
El Paso, TX 79927
(915) 858-1130
350 native Mexican, South American, and African cactus and succulent species. Seed list $1.

THE BANANA TREE, INC.
715 Northampton St.
Easton, PA 18042
www.banana-tree.com

email: faban@enter.net
*More than 1,000
species, mostly tropi-
cal. Catalog $2.*

BOOTHE HILL FARMS
921 Boothe Hill
Chapel Hill, NC
27514
(919) 967-4091
*Organically grown
wildflower seeds.
Catalog free.*

BOUNTIFUL GARDENS
18001 Shafer Ranch
Road
Willits, CA 95490
(707) 459-6410
*Nonprofit; 450 open-
pollinated vegetables,
flowers, herbs, and
grains. Catalog free.*

W. ATLEE BURPEE &
CO.
300 Park Avenue
Warminster, PA
18974
(800) 888-1447
www.burpee.com
*Wide range of flowers,
herbs, and vegetables,
both heirloom and
new cultivars. Catalog
free.*

D. V. BURRELL SEED
GROWERS CO.
P.O. Box 150
Rocky Ford, CO
81067
(719) 254-3318
*Full line of vegetables
and flowers, but
famous for its selec-
tion of melons. Cata-
log free.*

BUTTERBROOKE FARM
78 Barry Road
Oxford, CT 06478
(203) 888-2000
*Old-time open-polli-
nated vegetables,
organically grown
using biodynamic
methods. Seed list free
with SASE.*

COMPANION PLANTS
7247 N. Coolville
Ridge Road
Athens, OH 45701
(740) 592-4643,
www.frognet.net/
companion_plants
email: complants@
frognet.net
*Culinary, dye, medici-
nal, and aromatic
herbs. Catalog $3.*

THE COOK'S GARDEN
P.O. Box 535
Londonderry, VT

(800) 457-9703
*Vegetables, especially
salad plants, and flow-
ers; many choice
European cultivars.
Catalog free.*

CORNS
R-1, Box 32
Turpin, OK 73950
(405) 778-3615
*Nonprofit; heirloom
corn cultivars. Seed
list $1.*

WILLIAM DAM SEEDS
LTD.
Box 8400
Dundas, ON
L9H 6M1 Canada
(905) 628-6641
*Flowers and vegeta-
bles, especially Euro-
pean cultivars. Cata-
log $2.*

DEEP DIVERSITY
P.O. Box 15700
Santa Fe, NM 87505
(505) 438-8080
*1,500 open-pollinated
vegetables, flowers,
herbs, shrubs, grasses,
vines, and trees. Cata-
log $6.*

DEGIORGI SEED CO.
6011 N Street
Omaha, NE 68117

(402) 731-3901
2,000 annual and perennial flowers, vegetables, herbs, grasses and wildflowers, heirlooms and hybrids. Catalog free.

ELIXIR FARM BOTANICALS
General Delivery
Brixey, MO 65618
(417) 261-2393
Chinese and indigenous medicinals. Seed list free.

EVERGREEN Y.H. ENTERPRISES
P.O. Box 17538
Anaheim, CA 92817
(714) 637-5769
200 Asian vegetables and herbs. Catalog $2, refundable with order.

FEDCO SEEDS
P.O. Box 520
Waterville, ME 04903
Cooperative; 650 vegetables and flowers for cold, short seasons. Catalog $2.

FERRY-MORSE SEEDS
P.O. Box 1620
Fulton, KY 42041
(800) 626-3392

200 familiar vegetable, herb, and flower cultivars. Catalog free.

FIELD & FOREST PRODUCTS, INC.
N3296 Kuzuzek Road
Peshtigo, WI 54157
(715) 582-4997
Mushroom spawn. Catalog $2, refundable with order.

FILAREE FARM
182 Conconully Highway
Okanogan, WA 98840
(509) 422-6940
Garlic. Catalog $2, refundable with order.

THE FLOWERY BRANCH SEED CO.
P.O. Box 1330
Flowery Branch, GA 30542-1330
(770) 536-8380
1,900 annual and perennial flowers and herbs; large selection of cut flowers and everlastings. Catalog $4, refundable with order.

FOX HOLLOW SEED COMPANY
P.O. Box 148

McGrann, PA 16236
(888) 548-SEED
Heirloom vegetable, herb, and flower seeds. Catalog free.

THE FRAGRANT PATH
P.O. Box 328
Fort Calhoun, NE 68023
760 fragrant flowers, vines, and herbs. Catalog $2.

FROSTY HOLLOW ECOLOGICAL RESTORATION
P.O. Box 53
Langley, WA 98260
(360) 579-2332
email: wean@whidbey.net
Pacific Northwest wildflowers, grasses, shrubs, and trees. Seed list for SASE.

GARDEN CITY SEEDS
778 Highway 93 No.
Hamilton, MT 59840
(406) 961-4837
300 vegetable cultivars bred for cold climates; large selection of cover crops. Catalog free.

GARDENS NORTH
5984 Third Line Road North
North Gower, ON

K0A 2T0 Canada
(613) 489-0065.
email: garnorth@
istar.ca
Perennial flowers and grasses. Catalog $4.

THE GOURMET
GARDENER
8650 College Blvd.
Overland Park, KS
66210
(913) 345-0490
Gourmet vegetable and herb cultivars. Catalog free.

GURNEY'S SEED &
NURSERY CO.
110 Capital Street
Yankton, SD 57078
Wide selection of old and new vegetable and flower cultivars. Catalog free.

HARRIS SEEDS
P.O. Box 22960
60 Saginaw Drive
Rochester, NY 14692
(800) 514-4441
Vegetables, including many hybrid propri-etary cultivars bred by Harris. Catalog free.

HEIRLOOM SEED
PROJECT, Landis Val-ley Museum

2451 Kissel Hill Road
Lancaster, PA 17601
(717) 569-0401
extension 202
Open-pollinated and heirloom vegetables, herbs, and fruits. Cat-alog $4.

HEIRLOOM SEEDS
P.O. Box 245
West Elizabeth, PA
15088-0245
(412) 384-0852
Heirloom vegetables. Catalog $1, refund-able with order.

HOLLAND WILD-
FLOWER FARM
P.O. Box 328
Elkins, AR 72727
(501) 643-2622
Wildflowers and wild-flower mixes. Seed list free.

LE JARDIN DU
GOURMET
P.O. Box 75
St. Johnsbury Center,
VT 05863-0075
(802) 748-1446
Gourmet vegetable cultivars from Europe. Seed list 50¢.

THOMAS JEFFERSON
CENTER FOR HISTORIC

PLANTS, MONTICELLO,
P.O. Box 316
Charlottesville, VA
22902
Nonprofit; heirloom flowers and vegetables, many grown by Jeffer-son at Monticello. Catalog $1.

JOHNNY'S SELECTED
SEEDS
Foss Hill Road
Albion, ME 04910
(207) 437-9294
Flowers, herbs, and vegetables, many suit-ed to cool climates. Catalog free.

J. W. JUNG SEED CO.
335 South High St.
Randolph, WI 53957
(800) 247-5864
Flowers, herbs, and vegetables, both old and new cultivars. Catalog free.

KITAZAWA SEED CO.
1111 Chapman Street
San Jose, CA 95126
(408) 243-1330
Asian vegetables. Cat-alog free.

THE KUSA SEED
RESEARCH FOUNDATION
P.O. Box 761

Ojai, CA 93024
*Nonprofit; grains and
other food crops, most-
ly endangered culti-
vars. Catalog $2.50
and business SASE.*

D. LANDRETH SEED
COMPANY
P.O. Box 6426
Baltimore, MD 21230
*Old and new vegetable
and herb cultivars.
Seed list free.*

LIBERTY SEED CO.
P.O. Box 806
New Philadelphia,
OH 44663
(330) 364-1611
*1,000 vegetables and
flowers; many bedding
cultivars. Catalog
free.*

MELLINGER'S INC.
2310 W. South Range
Road
North Lima, OH
44452-9731
(216) 549-9861
*Familiar flower culti-
vars. Catalog free.*

MIDWEST WILDFLOWERS
P.O. Box 64
Rockton, IL 61072
*Wildflowers for the
Midwest. Catalog $1.*

MOON MOUNTAIN
WILDFLOWERS
P.O. Box 725
Carpinteria, CA
93014-0725
(805) 684-2565
*Wildflowers and wild-
flower mixes. Catalog $3.*

NATIVE SEEDS, INC.
14590 Triadelphia
Mill Road
Dayton, MD 21036
(301) 596-9818
*Wildflowers and wild-
flower mixes. Catalog
free.*

NATIVE SEEDS/
SEARCH
526 North 4th
Avenue
Tucson, AZ 85705
(520) 622-5561
*Nonprofit; traditional
southwestern food
crops and other heir-
loom vegetables. Cata-
log $1.*

NORTHPLAN/
MOUNTAIN SEED
P.O. Box 9107
Moscow, ID 83843-
(208) 882-8040
 email: norplan@
moscow.com
*Native grasses, flow-
ers, shrubs, vines, and*

*trees for reclamation
planting. Seed list for
business SASE.*

NORTHWEST MYCO-
LOGICAL CONSULTANTS
702 N.W. 4th Street
Corvallis, OR 97330
(541) 753-8198
*Mushroom spawn.
Catalog $2.*

P & P SEED COMPANY
14050 Route 62
Collins, NY 14034
(800) 449-5681
*Seeds for giant veg-
etable cultivars. Seed
list for business SASE.*

THEODORE PAYNE
FOUNDATION
10459 Tuxford Street
Sun Valley, CA 91352
(818) 768-1802
email: theodore-
payne@juno.com
*Nonprofit; more than
300 species of native
California plants.
Catalog $2.50.*

THE PEPPER GAL
P.O. Box 23006
Fort Lauderdale, FL
33307-3006
(954) 537-5540
*250 pepper cultivars.
Catalog free.*

PINETREE GARDEN
SEEDS
P.O. Box 300
New Gloucester, ME
04260
(207) 926-4112
850 flowers, vegetables, and herbs, both heirloom and hybrid. Catalog free.

PRAIRIE MOON
NURSERY
RR 3, Box 163
Winona, MN 55987
(507) 452-1362
Native flowers and grasses. Catalog $2.

PRAIRIE NURSERY
P.O. Box 306
Westfield, WI 53964
(800) 476-9453
Native flowers and grasses. Catalog free.

PRAIRIE OAK SEEDS
P.O. Box 382
Maryville, MO 64468
(660) 582-4084
102 annual and perennial flowers, grasses, and herbs for drying. Catalog $1.

PRAIRIE RIDGE
NURSERY/ CRM
ECOSYSTEMS
9738 Overland Road

Mt. Horeb, WI 53572
(608) 437-5245
Native flowers and grasses. Catalog $5, refundable with order.

RICHTER'S HERBS
357 Highway 47
Goodwood, ON
L0C 1A0 Canada
(905) 640-6677
700 medicinal, culinary, and ornamental herbs. Catalog free.

P. L. ROHRER & BRO.
P.O. Box 250
Smoketown, PA
17576
(717) 299-2571
400 vegetables and flowers, a mix of old and new. Catalog free.

SBE SEED CO.
3421 Bream Street
Gautier, MS 39553
(800) 336-2064
www.seedman.com
email: seedman@
seedman.com
6,000 varieties of tropical herbs, flowers, fruits, shrubs, vines, and trees. Catalog $1, refundable with order.

F.W. SCHUMACHER CO.
36 Spring Hill Road
Sandwich, MA 02563-
(508) 888-0659
Tree seeds. Catalog $1.

SEED SAVERS
EXCHANGE/
FLOWER AND HERB
EXCHANGE
3076 North Winn Rd.
Decorah, IA 52101
(319) 382-5990
Two nonprofit organizations; membership gives access to more than 10,000 old and endangered varieties of vegetables, fruits, herbs, and flowers from throughout the world. SSE membership $25, FHE membership $10, information on both free.

SEEDS BLÜM
HC33 Idaho City
Stage
Boise, ID 83706
(208) 344-9802
Open-pollinated vegetables, herbs, and flowers. Catalog $3.

SEEDS OF CHANGE
P.O. Box 15700
Santa Fe, NM 87506
(888) 438-8080

500 organically grown, open-pollinated vegetables and flowers; many heirlooms. Catalog free.

SEEDS TRUST–HIGH ALTITUDE GARDENS
P.O. Box 1048
Hailey, ID 83333
(888) 762-7333
Wildflowers, vegetables, medicinal and culinary herbs, and grasses for short seasons; many heirlooms. Catalog free.

SELECT SEEDS–
ANTIQUE FLOWERS
180 Stickney Hill Rd.
Union, CT 06076
(860) 684-9310
Old-fashioned flowers. Catalog $1.

SHEPHERD'S GARDEN SEEDS
30 Irene Street
Torrington, CT 06790
(860) 482-3638
Herbs, fragrant flowers, and gourmet vegetables, most from Europe. Catalog free.

SILVERHILL SEEDS
P.O. Box 53108
Kenilworth

Cape Town 7745
South Africa
27 (21) 762-4245
Seeds of South African plants. Catalog $2.

SOUTHERN EXPOSURE
SEED EXCHANGE
P.O. Box 170
Earlysville, VA 22936
(804) 973-4703
Vegetables and flowers, mostly heirlooms. Catalog $2, refundable with order.

STOCK SEED FARMS
28008 Mill Road
Murdock, NE 68407
(402) 867-3771
Native prairie grasses and wildflowers. Catalog free.

STOKES SEEDS, INC.
Box 548
Buffalo, NY 14240
(716) 695-6980
2,500 vegetables and flowers, including many proprietary cultivars. Catalog free.

TERRITORIAL SEED
COMPANY
P.O. Box 157
Cottage Grove, OR 97424
(541) 942-9547

500 vegetables, herbs, and flowers for the Pacific Northwest. Catalog free.

THOMPSON & MORGAN
P.O. Box 1308
Jackson, NJ 08527
(800) 274-7333
Flowers and a few vegetables, mostly from England. Catalog free.

TOMATO GROWERS
SUPPLY COMPANY
P.O. Box 2237
Fort Myers, FL 33902
(941) 768-1119
Tomato and pepper seeds. Catalog free.

TOTALLY TOMATOES
P.O. Box 1626
Augusta, GA 30903
(803) 663-0016
Tomato and pepper seeds. Catalog free.

VERMONT WILD-
FLOWER FARM
Route 7
Charlotte, VT 05445
(802) 425-3500
Native and other wildflowers. Catalog free.

WELL-SWEEP HERB FARM
205 Mt. Bethel Road
Port Murray, NJ
07865
(908) 852-5390
Herbs. Catalog $2.

WILD GARDEN SEED
Shoulder to Shoulder
Farm
P.O. Box 1509
Philomath, OR 97320
(541) 929-4068
*More than 200 wild
salad plants,
hedgerow plants,*

*native species, and
plants that attract
beneficial insects. Cat-
alog $4, refundable
with order.*

WILDGINGER WOOD-
LANDS
P.O. Box 1091
Webster, NY 14580
(716) 872-4033
*Northeast wildflowers
and ferns. Catalog $1,
refundable with order.*

WILDSEED FARMS
425 Wildflower Hills

P.O. Box 3000
Fredericksburg, TX
78624-3000
(409) 234-7353
*Wildflowers and wild-
flower mixes. Catalog
free.*

WILLHITE SEED, INC.
P.O. Box 23
Poolville, TX 76487
(817) 599-8656
*Hybrid and open-polli-
nated vegetables;
watermelon specialist.
Catalog free.*

FOR MORE INFORMATION

FURTHER READING

Abraham, Doc, and Katy Abraham. *Growing Plants from Seed*. Lyons & Burford, New York, 1991.

Ashworth, Suzanne. *Seed to Seed*. Seed Savers Publications, Decorah, Iowa, 1991.

Barton, Barbara. *Gardening by Mail*. 5th edition. Houghton Mifflin Company, Boston, 1997.

Bewley, J. Derek, and Michael Black. *Seeds: Physiology of Development and Germination*. 2nd edition. Plenum Press, New York, 1994.

Bir, Richard E. *Growing and Propagating Showy Native Woody Plants*. University of North Carolina Press, Chapel Hill, 1992.

Bubel, Nancy. *The New Seed-Starters Handbook*. Rodale Press, Emmaus, Pennsylvania, 1988.

Capon, Brian. *Botany for Gardeners: An Introduction and Guide*. Timber Press, Portland, Oregon, 1990.

Coleman, Eliot. *The New Organic Grower*. Chelsea Green Publishing Company, White River Junction, Vermont, 1995.

Cutler, Karan Davis. *Burpee: The Complete Vegetable & Herb Gardener*. Macmillan, New York, 1997.

DeBaggio, Thomas. *Growing Herbs from Seed, Cutting & Root*. Interweave Press, Loveland, Colorado, 1994.

Deno, Normal. *Seed Germination Theory and Practice*. 139 Lenor Drive, State College, Pennsylvania.

Dirr, Michael A. and Charles W. Heuser, *The Reference Manual of Woody Plant Propagation*. Varsity Press, Athens, Georgia, 1987.

Eldridge, Judith. *Cabbage or Cauliflower? A Garden Guide for the Identification of Vegetable and Herb Seedlings*. David R. Godine, Boston, 1984.

Ferreniea, Viki. *Wildflowers in Your Garden: A Gardener's Guide*. Random House, New York, 1993.

Halpin, Anne. *Foolproof Planting*. Rodale Press, Emmaus, Pennsylvania, 1990.

Harkness, Mabel G. *Seedlist Handbook*. 2nd edition. Timber Press, Portland, Oregon, 1993.

Huxley, Anthony. *Huxley's Encyclopedia of Gardening for Great Britain and America.* Universe Books, 1981.

Lloyd, Christopher, and Graham Rice. *Garden Flowers from Seed.* Timber Press, Portland, Oregon, 1994.

Loewer, Peter. *Seeds: The Definitive Guide to Growing, History & Lore.* Macmillan, New York, 1995.

Marinelli, Janet, ed. *The Brooklyn Botanic Garden Gardener's Desk Reference.* Henry Holt and Company, New York, 1998.

Marshall, Nina T. *The Gardener's Guide to Plant Conservation.* World Wildlife Fund, New York, 1993.

Phillips, Harry R. *Growing and Propagating Wild Flowers.* University of North Carolina Press, 1985.

Powell, Eileen. *From Seed to Bloom.* Storey Communications, Pownal, Vermont, 1995.

Raeburn, Paul. *The Last Harvest: The Genetic Gamble That Threatens to Destroy American Agriculture.* Simon & Schuster, New York, 1995.

Rogers, Marc. *Saving Seeds: The Gardener's Guide to Growing and Storing Vegetable and Flower Seeds.* Storey Communications, Pownal, Vermont, 1990.

Stein, Sara. *Planting Noah's Garden.* Houghton Mifflin Company, Boston, 1997.

Tenenbaum, Frances. *Taylor's Dictionary for Gardeners.* Houghton Mifflin Company, Boston, 1997.

Weaver, William Woys. *Heirloom Vegetable Gardening: A Master Gardener's Guide to Planting, Growing, Seed Saving, and Cultural History.* Henry Holt and Company, New York, 1997.

Whealy, Kent, *Garden Seed Inventory.* 4th edition. Seed Savers Exchange, Decorah, Iowa, 1995.

Wright, Robert, and Alan Titchmarsh. *The Complete Book of Plant Propagation.* Ward Lock, London, 1987.

Young, James A. and Cheryl G. Young. *Collecting, Processing, and Germinating Seeds of Wildland Plants,* Timber Press, Portland, Oregon, 1986.

Young, James A. and Cheryl G. Young. *Seeds of Woody Plants in North America.* Dioscorides/ Timber Press, Portland, Oregon, 1992.

PLANT & HORTICULTURAL SOCIETIES

Many plant and horticultural societies sponsor seed exchanges for their members. These organizations, which include an enormous variety of interests, are also one of the best sources for information about propagating plants from seeds.What follows is only a hint of of the help that is available; for a more complete listing of societies, consult *Brooklyn Botanic Garden Gardener's Desk Reference* (see page 101).

American Bamboo Society
750 Krumkill Road
Albany, NY 12203

American Begonia Society
157 Monument Road
Rio Dell, CA 95562

American Conifer Society
P.O. Box 360
Keswick, VA 22947-0360

American Dahlia Society
1 Rock Falls Court
Rockville, MD 20854

American Fern Society
326 West Street N.W.
Vienna, VA 22180

American Gourd Society
P.O. Box 274
Mt. Gilead, OH 43338

American Hibiscus Society
P.O. Box 12073W
St. Petersburg FL 33733-2073

Arizona Native Plant Society
P.O. Box 41206
Sun Station
Tucson, AZ 85717

California Horticultural Society
1847 34th Avenue
San Francisco, CA 94122-4109

The Canadian Wildflower Society
Unit 12A, Box 228
4981 Highway 7 East
Markham, ON L3R 1N1, Canada

Clivia Club
P.O. Box 74868
Lynwood Ridge
Pretoria, South Africa 0040

Cottage Garden Society
Clive Lane
Hurstfield House
244 Edleston Road
Crewe, Cheshire, England CW2 7EJ

United Plant Savers
P.O.Box 420
East Barre, VT 05649
medicinal plants

GARDENING ONLINE

Sites come and go with frustrating regularity, but the World Wide Web is nevertheless a remarkable and ever-expanding resource for backyard gardeners. Many Extension Service offices and state universities provide up-to-date information for gardeners in their regions. Of special value is the database of publications from 40 North American colleges and universities that is maintained by **Ohio State University** (www.hcs.ohio-state.edu/hcs/hcs.html).

There are scores of **U.S. Department of Agriculture** sites (the Department's home page is www.usda.gov), including the **Germplasm Resources Information Network** (www.ars-grin.gov) and the **National Agricultural Library** (www.nalusda.gov). Current and past weather information is available from the **National Weather Service** (www.nws.noaa.gov).

Many horticulture and garden organizations, such as the **Pennsylvania Horticultural Society** (www.libertynet.org/~phs), **Britain's Royal Horticultural Society** (www.rhs.org.uk), the **American Horticultural Society** (members.aol.com.gardenahs), and the **National Gardening Association** (www2.garden.org/nga) are online, as are dozens of botanic gardens, including **Brooklyn Botanic Garden** (www.bbg.org) and the **Royal Botanic Gardens, Kew** (www.rbgkew.org.uk).

Professional and trade organizations, including the **American Seed Trade Association** (www.amseed.com), the **International Plant Propagation Society** (www.ipps.org/ipps), and the **National Wildflower Research Center** (www.wildflower.org), have gone online, as have many plant societies, such as the **New England Wild Flower Society** (www.newfs.org/~newfs) and the **North American Rock Garden Society** (www.nargs.org). Dozens of seed companies also have web sites.

Three popular garden sites— **Garden Web** (www.gardenweb.com), **Garden Gate** (gardengate.infospace.com), and **GardenNet** (gardennet.com)—contain, in addition to proprietary features and information, hundreds of links to other garden sites.

You may also want to participate in a Usenet newsgroup for gardeners, such as rec.gardens, or sign up with one of several Listserv groups that specialize in gardening.

The author of *Seed to Seed* (Seed Saver Publications, 1991), SUZANNE ASHWORTH has been a volunteer curator—three acres of eggplants, gourds, and other vegetables—for Seed Savers Exchange for 12 years. She also works as a Preliterate Language Specialist for the Sacramento City Schools and teaches botany at American River College. She is currently studying the stability of the chemical constituents of herbs during storage.

MARILYN BARLOW is a seed merchant specializing in antique and heirloom flowers. Her mail order company, Select Seeds, is in Union, Connecticut.

JENNIFER BENNETT, who lives near Kingston, Ontario, is the author of eight gardening books and a regular garden column for *Canadian Living* magazine. Her most recent book is *Dry Land Gardening: A Xeriscaping Guide for Dry Summer, Cold Winter Climates* (Firefly, 1995).

KARAN DAVIS CUTLER, who gardens in the rationed warmth of northern Vermont, is the author of *Burpee: The Complete Vegetable & Herb Gardener* (Macmillan, 1997), which the Brooklyn Botanic Garden selected as one of its 1997 Best Garden Books of the Year. A former editor of *Harrowsmith Country Life* magazine, she has edited two other BBG handbooks, *Salad Gardens* (1995), which won the 1996 Quill and Trowel Award from the Garden Writers of America, and *Tantalizing Tomatoes* (1997).

DAVID J. ELLIS is the editor of *The American Gardener*, the official publication of the American Horticultural Society. In addition to developing a native woodland garden at his Silver Spring, Maryland, home, he maintains an heirloom tomato— "probably derived from the same stock as 'Brandywine'"—that has been in his family since at least the 1940s.

Horticulture writer and illustrator PETER LOEWER gardens near Asheville in the mountains of North Carolina. He is the author of many articles and books, including *Seeds: The Definitive Guide to Growing, History and Lore* (Macmillan, 1995). His most recent books are *The Winter*

Garden (Stackpole Books, 1997) and, with Jean Loewer, *The Moonflower* (Peachtree, 1997), an illustrated book for children.

HEATHER MCCARGO is a horticultural consultant and educator who specializes in the propagation and cultivation of native flora, plant conservation, organic horticulture, and natural garden design. She is the former plant propagator for the New England Wild Flower Society and currently lives in Maine, where she runs her business, Wildland Flora Consulting.

SHEPHERD OGDEN, who gardens in southern Vermont, is the founder of The Cook's Garden, a seed company specializing in vegetables, herbs, and flowers for the kitchen garden. A former market gardener, he is a frequent contributor to BBG handbooks and is the author of several garden books, including *Step by Step Organic Vegetable Gardening* (HarperCollins, 1992).

KENT WHEALY is the founder and director of Seed Savers Exchange, which today serves as the model for genetic preservation efforts in more than 30 countries. In 1990, he received a MacArthur Fellowship for his efforts to conserve genetic resources; he is also the recipient of Russia's prestigious N. I. Vavilov medal. SSE's Heritage Farm in Iowa maintains and displays more than 18,000 varieties of heirloom vegetables.

PHOTO CREDITS

Larsh Bristol: page 23.

David Cavagnaro: cover, pages 1, 4, 7, 20, 24, 26, 31, 32, 33, 36, 40, 41, 43, 45, 47 (top & bottom), 49, 50, 53, 54, 57, 58, 59, 65, 71, 75, 77, 81, 82, 84, 85, 87 (left, right & bottom), 89, 90, 91, 99, and 106.

Karan Davis Cutler: pages 68 and 73.

Alan & Linda Detrick: pages 8, 16, 18, 55, 60, and 62 (top & bottom).

Christine M. Douglas: page 66.

Susan M. Glascock: page 34.

Drawings by Peter Loewer: cover background, pages 12, 14, 15, 17, and 19.

"Plant kidney beans, if you be so willing,

When elm leaves are as big as a shilling.

When elm leaves are as big as a penny,

You must plant beans if you mean to have any."

TRADITIONAL RHYME

BROOKLYN BOTANIC GARDEN

21 ST-CENTURY GARDENING SERIES

for further information please contact the

BROOKLYN BOTANIC GARDEN

1000 Washington Avenue

Brooklyn, New York 11225

(718) 622-4433 ext. 265 www.bbg.org

Watch our garden grow in your very own mailbox!

From Great Neck to Great Bend, Big River to Little Creek, over 20,000 people in all 50 states enjoy the bountiful benefits of membership in the **Brooklyn Botanic Garden** – including our renowned gardening publications.

Brooklyn Botanic Garden Membership

The splendor that makes the Brooklyn Botanic Garden one of the finest in the world can be a regular part of your life. BBG membership brings you subscriptions to some of the liveliest, best-researched, and most practical gardening publications anywhere – including the next entries in our acclaimed 21st-Century Gardening Series (currently published quarterly). BBG publications are written by expert gardeners and horticulturists, and have won prestigious *Quill and Trowel* awards for excellence in garden publishing.

Plants & Gardens News – practical t and suggestions from BBG experts.

SUBSCRIBER $35
(Library and Institution Rate $60)
* A full year of *21st-Century Gardening Series* handbooks
* A year's subscription to *Plants & Gardens News*
* Offerings of Signature Seeds, handbooks and videos
* Reciprocal privileges at botanical gardens across the country

FAMILY/DUAL $50
All benefits of SUBSCRIBER, plus
* Membership card for free admission for two adult members and their children under 16
* 10% discount at the Terrace Cafe & Garden Gift Shop
* Free parking for four visits
* Discounts on classes, trips and tours

SIGNATURE $125
All benefits of FAMILY, plus
* Your choice of a Signature Plant from our annual catalog of rare and unique shrubs, perennials and house plants
* 12 free parking passes
* A special BBG gift calendar

BBG Catalog – quarterly listing of classes, workshops and tours in the and abroad, all at a discount.

SPONSOR $300
All benefits of SIGNATURE, plus
* Your choice of <u>two</u> Signature Plants
* Four complimentary one-time guest passes
* 24 free parking passes
* Invitations to special receptions

GARDENING BOOKS FOR THE NEXT CENTURY
Brooklyn Botanic Garden's 21st-Century Gardening Series explore frontiers of ecological gardening - offering practical, step-by-step tips on creating environmentally sensitive and beautiful gardens for the 1990s and the new century.

21st-Century Gardening Series – the handbooks in this acclaimed library.

Spring 1998
Please send in this form or contact BBG
for current membership information, higher levels and benefits.